THE CONDOR

Look for these and other books in the
Lucent Endangered Animals and Habitats Series:

The Amazon Rain Forest
The Bald Eagle
Bats
The Bear
Birds of Prey
The Cheetah
Coral Reefs
The Crocodile
Dolphins and Porpoises
The Elephant
The Giant Panda
The Gorilla
The Jaguar
The Manatee
The Oceans
The Orangutan
The Rhinoceros
Seals and Sea Lions
The Shark
The Tiger
The Whale
The Wolf

Other related titles in the Lucent Overview Series:

Endangered Species
Energy Alternatives
Environmental Groups
Garbage
Hazardous Waste
Oil Spills
Ozone
Population
Saving the American Wilderness
Zoos

THE CONDOR

BY KAREN D. POVEY

**Endangered
Animals &
Habitats**

LUCENT BOOKS, INC.

SAN DIEGO, CALIFORNIA

Library of Congress Cataloging-in-Publication Data

Povey, Karen, 1962–
    The condor/ by Karen Povey.
        p.   cm. — (Endangered animals & habitats)
    Includes bibliographical references (p.) and index.
        ISBN 1-56006-864-7 (hardback)
        1. California condor—Juvenile literature. 2. Endangered species—
    Juvenile literature. [1. California condor. 2. Condors. 3. Endangered
    species.] I. Title. II. Series.
        QL696.F33 P68 2001
        598.9'2—dc21

2001000067

Copyright © 2001 by Lucent Books, Inc.
P.O. Box 289011, San Diego, CA 92198-9011
Printed in the U.S.A.

Contents

Introduction

AMONG THE LARGEST birds ever to take flight, condors evolved at a time when North and South America provided a reliable banquet of plentiful food for the huge scavengers. Thousands of years ago great herds of large grass-eating animals were found on both continents. When these woolly mammoths, mastodons, camels, and bison died from disease or predation, their carcasses provided food for condors. In South America, the Andean condor soared over the peaks of the Andes Mountains from what is now Venezuela to the southern tip of Chile. The California condor, despite its present-day name, roamed with mammal herds over much of North America. Evidence indicates that California condors were once found in New York State, Florida, throughout the desert Southwest, northern Mexico, and as far north as southern Alaska.

The wide range of the Andean and California condors occurred ten thousand years ago, as the last ice age was ending. Around this time, the large mammals that the condor depended on for food were unable to adapt to the changing environment and began to disappear. As its food sources dwindled, the condor's range began to shrink. In South America, Andean condor numbers were severely reduced, especially in Colombia and Venezuela, the northernmost portion of their range.

California condors also suffered from this loss of food and disappeared from inland North America. The condors that remained became concentrated in the West, where food was still available. However, the arrival of Europeans in this region in the mid-1800s placed new pressures on the condor. Human activities and encroachment essentially sealed the fate of a bird whose range had already been dramatically reduced.

Direct persecution, through hunting and egg collection, as well as advancing human settlement in the West caused the California condor's population to decline rapidly. By the early 1900s only one hundred birds remained.

These numbers continued to drop until, by the 1980s, it was apparent that the condor was close to extinction. Only nine individuals remained in the wild; twenty-four more resided in zoos. All hope had faded that the condor population would recover without human intervention. Faced with the prospect of losing the species forever, the U.S. Fish and Wildlife Service examined the alternatives. One option was to do nothing: The birds remaining in the wild

The population of the California condor declined rapidly due to hunting, egg collection, and advancing human settlement.

would be left alone to continue their course toward extinction. The alternative was to remove the birds from the wild and use them as the basis for a captive-breeding program to reestablish the species.

In 1987 the decision was made to round up the last free-living condors to begin an ambitious plan of captive breeding and eventual reestablishment of a wild population. This decision ultimately led to one of the most costly and most controversial experiments ever undertaken to revive an endangered species.

Condors captured from the wild were taken to breeding facilities at the San Diego Wild Animal Park and the Los Angeles Zoo. Eventually, a third breeding site was established in Boise, Idaho, at the World Center for Birds of Prey. By 1991, fifty-two condors were in captivity, enough to begin releasing them into the wild. Condors were released first in southern California, then in Arizona, and most recently along the central California coast.

Although there have been setbacks, there is reason to be optimistic about the future of the condor. Released birds

Condors were released from these pens at Vermilion Cliffs, Arizona, as part of an attempt to reestablish the condor population in the wild.

are showing increased natural social behavior and will be old enough to breed within the next few years. It will take years for the condor population to become secure, but biologists are hopeful that the bird is well on its way to maintaining a presence in western North America.

Experts estimate that condor conservation efforts will eventually cost nearly $50 million, a large sum of money to be spent on an ungainly, prehistoric bird. Americans, however, have made a commitment to the endangered species program, and most herald the recovery efforts for the condor as being "the right thing to do." Hopefully, in the future the value of this program will be affirmed by the presence of a healthy free-living condor population.

1

Meet the Condor

THE SIGHT OF condors soaring on immense wings stirred deep emotions in early residents of the Western Hemisphere. Even today the Andean condor plays a prominent role in the folklore of numerous South American cultures, where, since the time of the ancient Incas, it has been considered sacred. To various native peoples of western North America, California condors were a source of supernatural power and played an important role in their legends and rituals. The Tlingit people of British Columbia, Canada, believed the condor flashed lightning from its eyes and created thunder by flapping its wings. The Central Miwok Indians of California performed the *moloku*, or condor dance. Members of the Chumash tribe believed the spirits of the dead were carried to the afterlife on the condor's wings. Many different tribes performed ritual sacrifices of condors. Afterward, the condor's feathers, skin, and bones would be used in ceremonies to communicate with the spirit world.

Today condors continue to inspire great admiration and awe. People fortunate enough to catch a rare glimpse of a wild condor describe it as a thrilling experience. Dick Smith, who has observed wild California condors for thirty years, offers his impression:

> To sense the close passage of a traveling condor is an experience out of this world . . . Suddenly he looms above you, peering down with age-old rather remote gaze . . . To feel the presence of that vast composure and to hear the rush and whistle of his feathers through the air, and to see him gone to

his home in the darkening east, having passed within a rope's cast of you, is something to be forever remembered.[1]

Seeing a condor in flight would undoubtedly leave a strong impression, because the California condor, officially named *Gymnogyps californianus*, is North America's largest bird and one of the largest flying birds in the world. Adult California condors have a nine-and-a-half-foot wingspan and weigh up to twenty-four pounds. Larger still is the Andean condor, or *Vultur gryphus*, with wings measuring ten-and-a-half-feet across and weighing up to thirty-three pounds.

Viewed up close, the California condor has a black beak, blackish feathers with a triangular white patch under each enormous wing, and a ruff of long black feathers around the neck. The skin on an adult California condor's bald head and neck is colored various shades of red, orange,

 ## Condors and Early People

Much evidence illustrates the relationship between humans and condors in prehistoric times. Dwight Simons describes this evidence in the book *Vulture Biology and Management*, edited by Sanford Wilbur and Jerome Jackson. By studying remains and artifacts, Simons has determined that the condor played an important role in the ceremonies and religious practices of Native Americans. In a shell mound near San Francisco Bay, a complete condor skeleton was found. "The bird had been buried in a shallow depression, purposely dug and covered over again. . . . The completeness of this skeleton suggests special or ritual burial." Simons also describes many artifacts made from condor bones: "The most common types of condor bone artifact are tube/whistles fashioned from long bones of the wing." He also describes rock art: "Rock art positively identified as representing a California condor occurs at Condor Cave. . . . Above the entrance to Condor Cave is a pictograph of a condor, apparently taking off." In this book, Simons also catalogues archaeological evidence from thirteen sites in Oregon and California.

Condor Classification

Scientists use a system of classification to determine the relationships of different bird species. By comparing characteristics such as behavior and anatomy, scientists can group together related birds. These large groups are called orders. All of the birds within an order share some common features and have descended from common ancestors. Within an order, birds are further split into smaller groups, called families. Birds in the same family are more closely related to each other than to birds in other families within their order.

Condors, like other vultures found in North and South America, are part of the family called Cathartidae. Until recently the Cathartid vultures were thought to be part of the order Falconiformes, or the diurnal (daytime-hunting) raptors. Raptors are birds such as eagles, hawks, and falcons that kill prey with their powerful feet and sharp talons. New research has shown, however, that despite a superficial resemblance to raptors, Cathartid vultures are not closely related to them at all. In fact, close examination of the anatomy and behavior of raptors and Cathartid vultures show very few features in common. Although these vultures do possess a meat-tearing beak, they lack the powerful feet and talons characteristic of raptors. Scientists now classify Cathartid vultures as members of the order Ciconiiformes, which also includes herons and storks. DNA studies have confirmed that these vultures are more genetically similar to other Ciconiiforms than they are to raptors.

pink, yellow, and blue. This skin may convey the bird's mood with the colors becoming even more vivid during times of excitement. Although males weigh slightly more than females, the sexes appear identical.

The Andean condor, in contrast, has a slightly darker head, a light gray beak, and a white ruff of neck feathers. This condor has no white underneath its wings; instead, the feathers on the tops of its wings, closest to its body, are white. Adult male Andean condors can be distinguished from females by a large fleshy crest, called a caruncle, that runs from the top of its head to the base of its beak.

Condors are part of the New World vulture family. These are the vultures found in North and South America and include the turkey vulture, black vulture, and king vulture. Other unrelated vultures are found in Africa, Asia, and Europe.

Feeding habits

Condors, like all vultures, are scavengers. Instead of killing their prey, they feed on the carcasses of dead animals, or carrion. Although some vultures use their highly developed sense of smell to locate a carcass, condors find their food by sight. Condors have excellent eyesight, which helps them see things on the ground from high in the sky. Once a potential meal is spotted, a condor will often circle high in the air above the carcass before landing

The condor, like all scavengers, feeds on the remains of dead animals.

to feed. This circling behavior may serve as a signal to other condors, guiding them to available food. Condors will also watch for the presence of other competing scavengers, such as turkey vultures, ravens, and golden eagles, to locate a nearby food source.

Once the condor alights on a carcass, it uses its sharp beak and powerful neck muscles to tear through the thick hide. The condor uses its large feet to brace itself against the carcass as it pulls off chunks of meat. A condor may eat up to four pounds of food at a time, which it holds in its crop, an extension of the esophagus in the bird's throat. After gorging in this manner, a condor will not have to eat again for three to four days.

Because it may take several days after the death of an animal for a condor to locate the carcass, the meat it finds is rarely fresh. Often, a condor's meal comes from an animal that has died from a serious illness. Consuming food in such a state of decay or disease would kill most animals, but because the acid in the condor's digestive tract is so strong, it can safely eat almost any meat. For this reason, the condor plays an important role in its ecosystem. By destroying deadly bacteria, it may help keep diseases from spreading.

The condor's scavenging lifestyle has led to an important adaptation: its distinctive bald head. (The California condor's scientific name, *Gymnogyps californianus*, means "the bald vulture of California.") When feeding, a condor will often reach far inside a carcass. If its head were feathered, it would quickly become matted with bits of blood and tissue, creating an environment in which bacteria could develop. A bald head will remain cleaner, and most bits of blood are easily removed when the bird preens and bathes. Any other remnants of the meal on the bird's head will quickly dry up in the sun.

While feeding, a condor will also spend a great deal of time with its legs and feet in contact with the carcass. To kill any bacteria its limbs may pick up, a condor (like other vultures) performs urohydrosis. During urohydrosis, a condor urinates on its own legs. The highly acidic and concentrated

The bald head of the condor may appear unattractive to humans, but it is well adapted to the bird's feeding habits.

urine will kill any bacteria found there. This process also helps cool the bird as the urine evaporates.

Although the condor's bald head and urohydrosis behavior may be considered strange and unattractive by human standards, they are superb adaptations for this scavenger's lifestyle and environment.

Condor flight

Because the availability of carrion is limited, scavenging birds like condors may have to travel long distances in search of food. The condor, however, is specially designed to be energy efficient as it flies. Its long, broad wings are suited for soaring rather than flapping flight. A condor soars using warm currents of uprising air called thermals. It spirals upward on these thermals to gain altitude and then glides long distances seeking another thermal to climb. Riding thermals requires the condor to use very little energy in flight. A condor may fly over a hundred miles at speeds up to eighty miles per hour with

Teratorn Vultures

As large as the living condors are, they are dwarfed by their prehistoric relatives known as the teratorns, or "monster birds." These extinct members of the condor family likely lived alongside the California condor in the late Pleistocene, a geologic time period covering the last 2 million years. The teratorns were the largest flying birds of all time; species ranged in size from thirty to fifty pounds and had wingspans of twelve to seventeen feet. Instead of soaring, these enormous birds are thought to have used flapping flight like herons or pelicans. Like the condor, teratorns were meat eaters. Instead of being scavengers, however, scientists believe they may have actively hunted, chasing their prey on the ground.

Teratorn vultures were the largest flying birds of all time.

hardly a beat of its wings as it glides from thermal to thermal. A condor is able to control its speed and direction in flight with both its broad tail and the long feathers, called primaries, on its wingtips. When soaring, the condor's wings produce a whistling sound as a result of the air flowing past these primary feathers. This whistle has been reported to be loud enough to hear from one hundred yards away in ideal conditions. Condors have been reported flying as high as twenty-four thousand feet, although they maintain a much lower altitude when searching for food, usually between five hundred and one thousand feet.

Although magnificent and graceful in the air, an earthbound condor is much more awkward and ungainly. After feeding on the ground, a condor must run while flapping its wings furiously for thirty to forty feet before its heavy body

The condor can adjust its flight speed and direction with its broad tail and long wing feathers.

can become airborne. Because of the difficulty of lifting its body off the ground, a condor will commonly roost on high perches along cliff faces, where it can easily become airborne with just a few wing beats. Tall dead trees are also favored roosting spots. Unless a condor is actively foraging or nesting, most of its time will be spent at a roost, a strategy that helps conserve energy.

Condor society

A condor spends much of its time at the roost sunning and preening its feathers. Sunning is most often performed in the morning as the condor prepares for the day's flight. The bird will spread its wings and orient itself to soak up the sun as directly as possible. Often, a condor will sun one side of its body, then turn to do the other. Preening, or grooming, of the feathers often accompanies sunning. A condor will spend hours running its beak through its feathers until they lay perfectly. During preening, a condor will also distribute oil throughout its plumage from a gland at

When sunning, the condor will spread out its wings to absorb the rays of the sun.

Condor Interactions with Other Birds

Condors share the western sky with a number of other large birds, including ravens, eagles, and turkey vultures. These birds may compete with condors for nesting and roosting sites and even for carcasses. As a result, sometimes interactions between condors and these other birds may turn aggressive. Dick Smith, an observer of wild condors in the 1960s and 1970s, witnessed some of these aggressive encounters and recounted them in his book *Condor Journal*:

> 10:47, bird is airborne and suddenly there is a second condor, both are soaring high, then down below us. An immature golden eagle is seen . . . they're attacking! Their wingbeats and dips and turns in the air were as fast as those of the eagle as they chased it. Eagle reached out legs and talons and condor swerved to avoid them. Condors finally drove eagle out of area.

Another journal entry describes a similar encounter:

> Seems the voyaging bird has returned. Now it chases away a raven, lands and then goes after a hawk. Condor from below joins it in air and now both are soaring. . . . I'm following the red-headed bird, with a fifth left primary missing. Aha! It's chasing a raven, now both are after it, right on it and the raven is ducking to get out of the way . . . fascinating to watch. Real vendetta against ravens, perhaps they are protecting a nesting area below.

the base of its tail. This oil is important for maintaining the feathers' waterproof capability.

The roost site is also where the social life of the condor is most apparent. Condors will perch together in groups with a great deal of interaction taking place between individuals. A strict social order, or hierarchy, is maintained in which certain birds are dominant over others. Maintaining this "pecking order" helps minimize aggressive conflicts that could result in injury. Instead of fighting, condors establish their hierarchy primarily through an extensive system of physical displays, including posturing with their heads and wings. Although condors have no syrinx, or voice box, they can communicate by making grunting and hissing sounds.

Condor reproduction

The roost is likely the scene of a condor's first encounter with its eventual mate. Once it reaches five or six years of age, a condor acquires a lifelong mate. (If a condor's mate should die, it will re-pair with another bird.) Condor pairs perform elaborate courtship rituals both on the ground and in flight. A male will court his partner by displaying with wings out, head down, and neck arched while slowly turning from side to side. This ritual is known as the courtship "dance." In the air, mates strengthen their bond by soaring together in graceful acrobatic displays.

Because it takes two years to raise a chick to independence, condors only breed every other year. Condor pairs select remote, inaccessible sites for their nests to assure that their eggs and chicks will be well protected from predators. Most often the nest will be located in a small cave on a cliff face or among boulders. Occasionally, nests will be in holes in large trees. Like most vultures, condors do not construct elaborate nests. Instead, they lay their ten-ounce, pale blue-green egg directly on the sand or gravel that has accumulated on the cliff ledge. Because it takes so much time and energy to raise a chick, only a single egg is laid. However, if the egg should break or be taken by predators, the pair will produce a replacement in about a month. This is known as double-clutching. Sometimes a pair will even produce a third egg if necessary. If, however, the loss of the egg occurs late in the breeding season, the pair will wait until the following year before breeding again.

Both parents share in the duties of caring for the egg. They take turns incubating the egg for two to five days at a time until it hatches fifty-four to fifty-eight days after being

laid. At first the chick is only partially covered in down, so the parents brood it constantly, covering the chick with their bodies to keep it warm. Later, as it develops a second coat of woolly, gray down feathers, its parents will warm the chick only during the night. For the first few weeks of life, the chick is fed several times a day by its parents, who re-gurgitate meat carried back to the nest in their crops. As the chick grows and can eat larger meals, the parents feed it only once a day. The chick, although still covered only in down and extremely awkward, will begin venturing out of the nest when it is eight weeks old.

By six months of age, the young condor's down has been replaced by its first set of flight feathers. With en-couragement from its parents, the juvenile bird is now able to take to the air. The first flights and landings are unsteady and clumsy as the chick learns to maneuver its huge wings. Eventually, as the chick gains experience and confidence,

Condors develop a full coat of down shortly after hatching.

it will accompany its parents on longer and longer flights. Although it can fly well by the time it is a year old, a juvenile condor relies on its parents through its second year, during which time it learns to locate food.

A juvenile condor is entirely dark in color, with black feathers and dark skin on its head and neck. After its third year, a young condor will begin the transition to the plumage and coloration of the adult. This change occurs gradually, as each year feathers are replaced during its molt. The adult pattern is established when the condor is sexually mature—roughly at the age of six—and is ready to find a mate of its own. Condors are thought to have a twenty-year life span in the wild. Captive condors, however, are known to live even longer. A condor kept at the National Zoo in Washington D.C., died at the age of forty-five.

A juvenile condor can be distinguished by its black feathers and by the dark skin on its head and neck.

The condor's long transition from chick to adult is perhaps the single most important reason for the endangerment of these remarkable birds. A young bird gaining independence is extremely vulnerable to both natural and human-influenced dangers, and many juveniles die before reaching maturity. It is therefore difficult for an adult condor pair, through the course of their lives, to rear even a single chick that successfully becomes a breeding adult itself. This slow rate of reproduction makes it especially hard for both California and Andean condor populations to recover from population declines. If condors are to survive, it will be essential for people to take an active role in minimizing the perils they face.

2

The Decline of the Condor

IT WILL NEVER be known how many California condors soared over North America in prehistoric times. Fossil records reveal, however, that condors once ranged widely over much of the continent. Evidence indicates that condors were found throughout the southern United States as far east as Florida and once nested in Texas, Arizona, and New Mexico. Fossil discoveries also reveal that condors once even lived in New York State. Over time, though, the condor's far-flung range began to shrink, eventually becoming just a tiny fraction of what it once was. By the early 1980s the range of this previously widespread bird was limited to just a six-county area north of Los Angeles, California.

Despite extensive study, the reasons for the condor's decline are still poorly understood. Most researchers agree that condors have been affected by a complex combination of both natural and human-caused factors. Natural changes in the environment were likely responsible for the first drops in condor numbers. This initial decline was later increased by the impact of people on the environment and on the condors themselves. To understand the effect these factors have had on condor populations, it is helpful to follow this bird's path through time.

Condors in prehistory

For most of the last one hundred thousand years, the California condor flew over an abundant North American landscape, dining on a steady food supply of prehistoric animals. This wide range occurred near the end of the geologic period called the Pleistocene. The end of the Pleistocene was also a time of global climate change. As the last ice age ended and the climate began to warm, the large mammals that the condor depended on for food began to die off. As its food sources dwindled, the condor's range did as well. Fossil evidence from Arizona, New Mexico, and Texas shows that condors disappeared from those inland areas ninety-five hundred years ago.

About the same time that the North American climate was changing, early humans arrived on the continent. Their influence on the condor's decline is greatly debated among scientists. Some believe that the impact of their hunting activities further accelerated the disappearance of large mammals, which directly resulted in the disappearance of condors. Others, however, believe that hunting by these relatively small numbers of people had little ill effect.

Europeans discover the condor

The influences of a changing environment and possible pressures from humans resulted in a dramatic decrease in the range of the condor. By the time history was first recorded in western North America, the condor was restricted to a narrow range along the Pacific coast from British Columbia, Canada, to Baja California, Mexico. These populations were likely fairly stable when the first European explorers arrived in the early seventeenth century. The fascination these explorers expressed toward condors was an early hint of the profound effect human attention would ultimately have on their survival. For instance, Father Antonio de la Ascensión, a Spaniard exploring the coast of California, wrote detailed observations of the animal life he encountered on his travels and made the first recorded observations of the California condor in 1602: "There are some other birds of the shape of turkeys, the largest I saw on this voyage. From the point of one wing to that of the other it was found to measure seventeen

Rancho la Brea

Deep within the heart of the bustling city of Los Angeles lies one of the best resources for information on the life of Pleistocene carnivores. Rancho la Brea, or "the Tar Ranch," was discovered by explorers in 1769. The expedition found a large marshy area that bubbled with a sticky substance, later learned to be asphalt. This asphalt is the result of underground oil deposits being slowly forced up through cracks in the earth.

Rancho la Brea, or the La Brea Tar Pits, as the site is more commonly known, has since been discovered to contain a rich fossil record of extinct animals from the last ice age, which were preserved in the asphalt from forty to ten thousand years ago. The remains of mammoths, saber-toothed cats, and early condors are among the fossils found there. In fact, since 1906 more than 1 million bones have been recovered. Of particular interest to scientists still excavating the site are the large numbers of remains from carnivorous animals. Scientists speculate that predators and scavengers were attracted to the site when large prey animals became mired in the sticky asphalt. As they attacked the animals or fed on the carcasses of ones already dead, the carnivores themselves became trapped. This cycle continued until large numbers of meat-eating animals had followed their intended victims in a slow, sticky death.

The La Brea Tar Pits contain rich fossil records of extinct animals from the last ice age.

spans [eleven feet, three inches]."[2] As more explorers visited the West in the nineteenth century, condor sightings became more frequent. The Lewis and Clark Expedition provided the first American observation of live condors along the Columbia River in Oregon in 1805. It recorded one individual weighing twenty-four pounds and called it "the beautiful buzzard of Columbia."[3]

Not everyone encountering condors considered them beautiful; many Europeans arriving in the West looked upon the big bird with fear and disgust. These settlers often considered the condor an omen of death, especially as they

Some scientists believe that the disappearance of large animals such as the mastodon contributed to the condor's decline.

watched the great birds circling over their next meal. The unusual appearance and gory feeding habits of condors only served to reinforce these perceptions.

The path of decline

Ultimately, many of the Western explorers and pioneers who encountered condors responded by shooting them. This was sometimes done out of curiosity or for sport. More often, however, ranchers who mistakenly thought condors were a threat to their livestock would shoot them on sight. Condors are naturally curious birds and were often approachable by those intent on causing them harm. Condor nests, too, became a target for professional egg hunters, who could sell the eggs to collectors for large sums. Collectors also sought condors that were shot and stuffed for use as museum specimens. In fact, at least 130 specimens are known to exist in museums around the world.

Besides facing pressure from hunting, California condors continued to experience a decrease in their food supply. During the last two hundred years, as people settled the West, wild animals became less abundant. Condors were forced to switch primarily to a diet of cattle, sheep, and horses that they found dead on rangelands. As ranchers began to better manage their herds and concentrated their stock on feedlots, even this food source became scarcer. This decreased availability of food is generally considered to be a prime factor in the California condor's decline.

In South America, Andean condors have fared slightly better than their cousins to the north in regard to their food supply. Although these condors also feed on the carcasses of domestic animals, they have a greater supply of wild animals such as deer, guanacos, and vicuñas (wild relatives of the domestic llama) to eat. Many condors live along the Pacific coast of South America, where they are able to feed on beached whales, sea lions, and fish.

In North America, hunting and the effects of rapid population growth greatly decreased condor numbers. In the 1880s, California passed legislation protecting condors, but it appeared to have little effect. The law was vague, referring only to "non-game" bird species, and was almost never enforced. By the early 1900s, the condor was restricted to a horseshoe-shaped range in southern California that was likely home to no more than one hundred birds. Over the course of the last half of the twentieth century, condor numbers continued to drop at the rate of two to four birds per year. One estimate indicated that there were fifty to sixty birds in the early 1960s. Because the condor population had become so small, the U.S. Fish and Wildlife Service listed the bird as an endangered species in 1967. By the late 1970s, only twenty-five to thirty remained.

Ongoing threats to the condor

Halting the decline of an endangered species requires an understanding of the threats it faces. While some of the early threats to the condor, such as egg collecting and sport hunting, are no longer of great concern, other serious problems

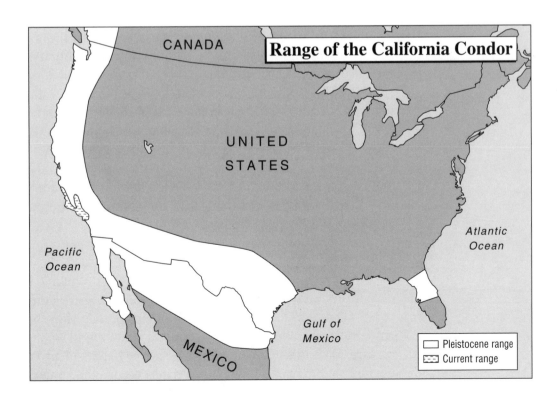

remain. Random shooting, poisoning, exposure to pesticides, and human disturbance and alteration of condor habitat all play varying roles in the condor's struggle for survival. Some of these factors affect the condor's ability to reproduce successfully while others directly cause the death of individual birds. However, because the bodies of few dead condors have ever been retrieved from the wild, it is extremely difficult for scientists to accurately assess the impact of each factor on overall condor mortality. As a result, scientists must often resort to making educated guesses about the best courses of action to protect the condor.

Shooting

It is known, however, that for centuries a leading cause of condor deaths was gunshot. In the 1800s and early 1900s, condors were popular targets for hunters obtaining skins or feathers for museum collections. Ranchers, not understanding the condor's role as a scavenger, would shoot birds found feeding on the carcasses of lambs and calves. In more recent times, as the public became more aware of the plight of the condor, these types of killings decreased dramatically. Even with increased publicity, though, condors remained the occasional targets of random shootings. Carl Koford, a prominent condor biologist, estimated that in the 1940s one condor a year died in this fashion. Examination of four condors found dead in the 1980s showed one to have been a victim of gunshot. Since condors gained legal protection in the 1880s, however, only one person was prosecuted and convicted for killing a condor: In 1908 a man was fined fifty dollars for shooting a condor in Los Angeles County, California.

Poisoning

Although the shooting of condors may always remain an occasional problem, of greater concern to biologists is the birds' exposure to the carcasses of other animals shot by hunters. Mammals such as deer, coyotes, and ground squirrels are sometimes hunted with lead shot or bullets in areas where condors live. Injured animals may escape the hunter, eventually die, and be eaten by condors. The ingestion of lead fragments from these carcasses can eventually lead to severe lead poisoning.

To determine the effects of lead exposure on condor mortality, Stanley Wiemeyer and his colleagues at the Patuxent Wildlife Research Center in Maryland conducted a study of environmental contaminants in four wild California condors found dead between 1980 and 1986. Three of the four birds were found to have died as a result of poisoning from the ingestion of lead. Similar studies have led to the conclusion that lead exposure is a significant problem for condors and may have been a major factor in their declining populations. Condors may also suffer from exposure to other environmental toxins such as the heavy metals copper, nickel, and chromium, but further studies are necessary to make this determination.

Condors' exposure to poison is not limited to toxic elements such as lead. Historically, ranchers throughout the condor's habitat frequently used poisons such as strychnine and cyanide to control coyote and rodent populations on rangeland. Some such poisons are still in use today and are administered through the use of bait or devices that eject poison when bitten. According to the U.S. Fish and Wildlife Service, "Deaths from one or more range poisons, including strychnine and various rodenticides, may have occurred historically, but convincing documentation of the occurrence and magnitude of such losses has not been documented."[4] Cyanide poisoning was found to be the cause of death in the fourth condor examined in Wiemeyer's study, although this was considered to be an unusual event. In another unusual poisoning, a condor died after ingesting ethylene glycol as a result of drinking antifreeze.

DDT

Of all contaminants found in the condor's environment, it is likely that none played a more significant role in the condor's decline than the pesticide dichloro-diphenyl-trichloroethane (DDT). DDT is an insecticide that was used extensively in the United States to control mosquitoes and other insect pests from the 1940s through the early 1960s. Although DDT did provide effective insect control, it also caused serious damage to the environment that was only discovered after decades of use. DDT persists in the environment for long periods of time, allowing ample time for animals to be exposed to its effects. Once ingested by an animal and metabolized, DDT breaks down into a highly toxic compound called dichloro-diphenyl-ethylene (DDE).

The extensive use of DDT to control pests has caused damage to the condor's environment.

Studies have shown that DDE played a significant role in the decline of many species of meat-eating birds, including bald eagles, peregrine falcons, brown pelicans, and condors. Birds with high levels of DDE in their bodies laid eggs with extremely thin shells, which would break under the weight of the incubating parent. As a result, many pairs of these birds were unable to successfully reproduce for years or even decades. It was not until 1972, when biologists determined the profound effect that DDT was having on bird populations, that the use of this pesticide was banned in the United States. Although it is impossible to look back and assess the true impact DDT had on the decline of condors, it is likely to have been a serious factor in the 1950s and 1960s.

Changing condor habitat

Once scientists understood the dangerous effects of pesticides on the condor's environment, they were able to take steps to improve the situation, such as banning DDT. Other changes to the condor's environment have proven more difficult, if not impossible, to solve. Humans have had a profound influence on the North American landscape, altering it permanently in many ways. The creation of obstacles, increased human disturbance, and loss of habitat have presented significant challenges to the survival of condors, and many other species of wildlife.

Much of the range preferred by condors is also highly desired by people. Vacation homes, ranches, mines, and oil rigs are scattered throughout condor habitat. Some manmade structures, such as power lines, become especially dangerous obstacles. Condors may have difficulty seeing lines spread across the sky and may accidentally fly into them. Several have been killed in collisions like these, suffering broken bones and skull fractures. Other birds, attempting to land on power poles, have been electrocuted when their wings touched the high-voltage lines.

Most of the effects of human settlement in condor country, however, are not as obvious or as easy to assess. For decades scientists have debated whether condors are harmed by the mere presence of humans in their territory. Some people once thought that if a condor spotted a person, it would leave that area permanently. Similarly, if a person disturbed nesting condors, it was said they would abandon the nest and never breed again. These extreme views have since been disproved, but questions remain about the impact human disturbance has on condors. Scientists believe that nesting condors are most sensitive and should be given as much seclusion as possible. Roosting birds seem to be less affected by human activity.

Also under debate is the importance of habitat loss as a factor in the condor's decline in recent history. While habitat loss has played a significant role in the endangerment of many species, the California condor actually has much of its most critical habitat still intact. Early attempts to protect condors led to the preservation of large tracts of wilderness in southern California for their nesting, roosting, and foraging activities. Condor biologists William Toone and Michael Wallace downplay the impact of habitat loss on the condor: "Considering the historical range of the condor, the nearly pristine conditions of its nesting habitat, and the fact that its foraging habitat has changed little over the last 100 years, it is difficult to place the full weight of the decline on a loss of habitat."[5] In fact, all of the condor nesting sites in the last four decades were located on public lands within the Los Padres, Angeles, and Sequoia National Forests.

The Andean condor

Although most of its range is more remote than that of the California condor, the Andean condor faces many of the same threats. Historically, the Andean condor ranged the length of western South America, from Colombia to southern Argentina. Today, however, its range has been considerably reduced. While still fairly abundant in Peru and areas along the southern coast of South America, condor numbers have declined greatly to the north. The last recorded breeding of condors in Venezuela occurred in the early 1900s. In Colombia, a small number of condors remains in high, isolated mountain areas.

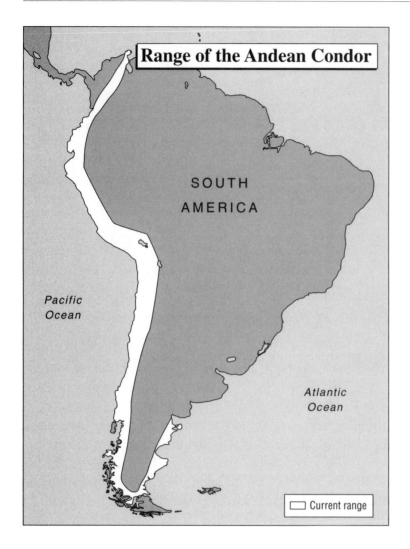

Range of the Andean Condor

SOUTH
AMERICA

Pacific
Ocean

Atlantic
Ocean

☐ Current range

Andean condors face the same kinds of persecution by people that caused the decline of their California cousins a century earlier. Hunting for feathers and bones, shooting for sport, and disturbance of nesting habitat have seriously affected the numbers of Andean condors. Additionally, until recently condors were still captured for use in festivals and ceremonies by native people in South America. To make matters worse, pesticides such as DDT, which have been banned in the United States, are still used in much of Latin America. Evidence of exposure to these chemicals has been found in Andean condors. All of these threats

The Andean condor population is diminishing due to hunting, disturbance of nesting habitat, and the use of pesticides.

may cause the Andean condor to follow the path of California condor.

Time to act

Although Andean condors may also have needed help, by the early 1970s time was becoming critical for the California condor. Although many questions remained about the reasons for their declining populations, one thing was certain: As a result of human activity and environmental changes, condors were disappearing fast. Ecologist David Brower bluntly sums up the plight of the condor: "When the vultures watching your society begin to drop dead, it's time to pause and wonder."[6] The time had come to take action to prevent the extinction of the California condor.

3

The California Condor Recovery Progam

ALTHOUGH THEIR NUMBERS had been low for decades, condors did not begin to receive official government attention until the 1930s. In 1933, the U.S. Forest Service attempted the first series of censuses, or counts, of condors in the Los Padres National Forest in southern California, the site of the largest remaining condor population. These condor counts were difficult due to the tendency of the birds to travel great distances each day. Care had to be taken to ensure that the same bird was not being counted twice. Because the condors were known to concentrate their activity at certain points within the forest, an observer would be stationed at each point and would record the date, time, and numbers of condors seen there. By comparing notes on the times the birds were observed, the counters could be certain that they were not tallying the same condors. In 1936 the National Audubon Society began its first direct involvement with condor preservation, providing the funds to continue paying for observers to count them.

Condor sanctuaries

The report of the 1937 Los Padres census estimated that the condor population consisted of between fifty-five and sixty birds. Armed with this information, the U.S. Forest

Service took the first step toward protecting the condor by creating the Sisquoc Condor Sanctuary that same year. The twelve-hundred-acre protected area encompasses an area in Los Padres National Forest that contains an important condor roost, nest site, and bathing pool. The Sisquoc Condor Sanctuary has been maintained to this day, and no one is allowed to enter unless he or she receives a special permit.

In 1939 Carl Koford of the Museum of Vertebrate Zoology at the University of California at Berkeley began the first scientific study of the remaining 150 California condors. His study, which continued through 1946, documented the first verifiable data on the condor's biology. Koford established the condor's need for appropriate foraging, roosting, bathing, and nesting sites. The National Audubon Society published his research results in 1953. Largely as a result of Koford's findings, a second refuge for condors, the Sespe Condor Sanctuary, was established in 1947, also in Los Padres National Forest. Originally thirty-five thousand acres, the Sespe Condor Sanctuary

Carl Koford

In his 1953 book *The California Condor*, Carl Koford voiced his frustration with pessimistic predictions of the condor's future. Although his words were written decades before, they still rang true for biologists working to save the condor in the 1980s:

Inasmuch as the condor has persisted in spite of apathy and predictions of its early extinction, let us be optimistic and assume that the species will persist indefinitely if we will give it aid. In the course of the past 60 years, the attitude of those who have written about condors has been mainly one of pessimism and of resignation to the approaching extinction of the species . . . Pessimism leads to apathy and defeatism. The major obstacle to all attempts to aid the condor has been the disinterest of persons capable of effective action.

was expanded to fifty-three thousand acres of protected habitat in 1951. Like the Sisquoc sanctuary, access to the Sespe sanctuary is restricted, except for two hiking trails that pass through.

With the creation of these sanctuaries, portions of condor habitat now had protection, but it was not until 1953

The Sespe Condor Sanctuary affords the condor fifty-three thousand acres of protected habitat.

The Endangered Species Act

In 1973 the federal government passed the Endangered Species Act (ESA) in an attempt to protect America's rarest plant and animal species. The ESA provides for the conservation of the entire ecosystems upon which endangered and threatened species depend. A detailed recovery plan is required for every species on the official list, which now numbers over nine hundred. Becoming listed involves a lengthy process of determining whether a species meets the legal definition of endangered or threatened. An endangered species is a plant or animal that is likely to become extinct in all or most of its range. A threatened species is one likely to become endangered in the near future. The ESA has been an important legal tool for providing protection for some of America's most remarkable wildlife, including the grizzly bear, bald eagle, and gray wolf. Because it protects the entire ecosystems in which these creatures live, thousands of other species receive protection as well.

Although environmentalists applaud the intent of the ESA, the flaws of the process are readily apparent. More than thirty-seven hundred species are currently proposed for listing, but a lack of funding, administrative difficulties, and political pressure form obstacles to the process. Some of the species waiting to be listed have likely already become extinct. Of the species that have made it to the list, 40 percent still await recovery plans. Furthermore, it is difficult and expensive to implement most of the recovery plans; to date, only a handful of species have recovered enough to be removed from the list.

A move is currently underway to revise the ESA to less strictly dictate the use of protected ecosystems. Business interests and many citizens' groups often oppose the restrictions put in place by the ESA. Some people hope to find ways to compromise to protect endangered species so that development and economic opportunities are not lost. Others hope to dramatically weaken or even discard the ESA completely. The future of America's endangered species may depend on the course the ESA takes.

that a law was enacted giving full legal protection to the condors themselves. The California condor was included on the first federal list of endangered species in 1967, and in 1971 it was protected through the California Endangered Species Act. Because of its extreme rarity, the condor was already well protected by law when Congress passed the federal Endangered Species Act (ESA) in 1973. All of these laws meant that it was illegal to collect or harm a condor in any way.

Passing laws to protect condors was relatively easy. The real work lay ahead—learning more about condors and determining the best strategy to halt their continued decline. In 1965 the U.S. Fish and Wildlife Service began the first full-time research on condors through the Patuxent Wildlife Research Center in Maryland. One of the first studies initiated was a comprehensive annual condor survey in which biologists estimated the population's numbers and ages. This survey demonstrated an alarming trend: Condor numbers were declining steadily. Most disturbing was the bird's extremely low reproduction rate. No more than two chicks per season had been hatched. By 1976 only forty condors remained.

Critical habitat concept

To improve the desperate situation of the condor, the first condor recovery plan was adopted in 1975. This comprehensive management plan was created in cooperation with both private and governmental agencies, including the U.S. Fish and Wildlife Service, the Bureau of Land Management, the U.S. Forest Service, the California Department of Fish and Game, and the National Audubon Society. This initial condor recovery plan focused on preserving habitat to halt the condor's decline.

Certain areas within traditional condor range were designated as critical habitat. These were areas considered to be crucial to the condors' nesting, roosting, and foraging activities. Parts of six southern California counties, encompassing 570,400 acres, were given this designation. The ESA prohibits any destruction or alteration of habitat that may negatively affect condors within this critical habitat area.

A controversial plan

Despite all of the efforts to rescue the condor through the creation of reserves and affording them legal protec-

Cooperating to Save the Condor

The condor recovery program is an example of the high degree of cooperation necessary to solve complex environmental problems. Public and private agencies as well as private individuals participated in making the recommendations and policies that attempted to save the California condor. Government agencies, zoos, conservation organizations, ranchers, biologists, and veterinarians are all part of the diverse group working toward condor recovery.

Public and private agencies as well as individuals participate in the effort to save the condor.

tion, the bird's numbers continued to drop. By 1979, with only twenty-five to thirty birds left, it was becoming clear that it would take a more drastic approach to save the condor from extinction. A team of experts from various government agencies and private organizations concerned with the condor's plight developed a new, more aggressive recovery plan. Their proposal consisted of two components: hands-on research of birds in the wild and the development of a captive-breeding program leading to the eventual release of zoo-raised birds into the wild.

Although many people saw this new plan as the last, best hope for the future of the condor, it was not without opponents. Some members of the conservation community were strongly critical of any plan that called for interfering with condors. They recommended an approach that left condors alone and instead focused on habitat preservation and public education. These people were optimistic that the condor population could still recover if humans gave more effort to eliminating the condor's environmental hazards and persecution.

Some of the most vocal opponents were against the plan for primarily moral reasons. Koford, one of the first biologists to study the condor, was strongly opposed to a captive-breeding program. "The beauty of a California condor is in the magnificence of its soaring flight. A condor in a cage," he wrote, "is uninspiring, pitiful, and ugly to one who has seen them soaring over the mountains."[7]

Another outspoken critic of the plan was David Brower, who at the time was the leader of the environmental organization Friends of the Earth. He, too, opposed confining condors to cages in a zoo. He argued that the condor had been on a steady, natural progression toward extinction since the end of the last ice age, ten thousand years ago. To him, the condor was a relic of a time long past and should be allowed to "die with dignity."[8]

Proponents of the recovery plan perceived the situation differently and countered Brower's argument. Although they agreed that the beginning of the condor's decline in prehistoric times was not caused by humans,

Proponents of the condor recovery program believe that hands-on research and captive breeding will help save the bird from extinction.

the more recent drops in population numbers definitely were. Because people harmed condors by shooting and poisoning them, it was a moral responsibility to do everything humanly possible to save them. To these advocates, the possibility of helping condors by placing them in captivity outweighed any ethical questions about doing so. Clearly, the plan to save the condor was not a sure thing; it was a last-ditch effort to save a species on the brink of extinction.

Can captive breeding succeed?

While these moral issues were being debated, there was also strong disagreement about the possibility for success of a captive-breeding program. Opponents of captive breeding were concerned that this plan would actually speed the condor's decline because of the risk of injury or death during the capture of birds from the wild. Even if birds were captured safely, it was unknown if breeding would occur in captivity. Of greatest concern, though, was the effect of the young condor's long dependence on its parents. Would condors hatched and raised in captivity be able to survive when released? How would they know where to look for food? Would they be able to form pairs and themselves breed one day?

Although the answers to these and many other questions remained uncertain, proponents were optimistic that captive breeding could succeed. The San Diego Zoo had already successfully established a captive-breeding program for the Andean condor. This program produced eleven chicks in the course of nine years. Because of the similar biology of Andean and California condors, zoo staff hoped to apply what they had learned about raising Andean condors to the California condor project.

Studying the condor

Both sides continued to argue about the best course of action to rescue the condor, but plans were moving ahead. Experts from the government agencies and the National Audubon Society enthusiastically endorsed the new strategy. Because the condor is an endangered species, it required an act of Congress to grant the team of experts special permission to proceed. In May 1980 the U.S. Fish and Wildlife Service and the California Department of Fish and Game granted the permits necessary to begin capturing birds. The U.S. Fish and Wildlife Service and the National

Audubon Society established the Condor Research Center in Ventura, California, to carry out the plan.

One of the center's first field projects was to conduct condor photo-censusing. Using this method, researchers examined photographs of condors in flight and thereby identified individual birds by the patterns of their feathers. This meant that biologists could now count condors reliably and, more importantly, determine relationships and interactions between birds.

In addition to the census work, hands-on study of condors also began. Researchers hoped to learn more about the condor's biology by capturing birds and fitting them with tags and radio transmitters in order to track them when released. The few remaining nesting pairs would also be studied. Any chicks produced would be examined, weighed, and tagged. These plans were just underway when, only one month later, tragedy struck. A young chick died, likely as a result of stress, while being examined by a team of biologists from the Condor Research Center. This event reinforced critics' fears that studying condors in this manner would harm them more than it would help them. The California Department of Fish and Game revoked all research permits while it investigated the matter.

By 1981, reassured that condors could be captured and handled safely, the Department of Fish and Game granted permission to the U.S. Fish and Wildlife Service to resume their research. The agency also agreed to allow the San Diego Wild Animal Park and the Los Angeles Zoo to establish captive-breeding programs, granting permits to capture three condors.

Double-clutching

In 1982, shortly after research resumed, biologists made a significant discovery. They observed a pair of condors that accidentally knocked their egg off their nest ledge during a squabble. Forty days later another egg was laid to replace the one that was lost. Although this double-clutching had been observed in Andean condors, this was the first recorded occurrence for a California condor pair. This

finding was critically important for the establishment of the captive-breeding program. Eggs could be taken from the nests of wild condors without affecting the birds' ability to raise chicks. Because condors normally raise only one chick every two years, by double-clutching and rearing

Double-clutching was first observed in California condors in 1982.

48

Condor biologists suggested that all wild condors be bred in captivity after six of the fifteen remaining wild condors disappeared during the winter of 1984–1985.

one egg in captivity, biologists can effectively double the number of young the parents could rear on their own.

In 1983 four eggs were taken from the wild and brought for hatching to the San Diego Zoo. Three of the four pairs that provided the eggs laid replacements. However, because the replacement eggs were laid much later in the year than they would normally have been, the resulting

chicks were destined to hatch late in the fall. These chicks, then, would likely still be dependent on their parents when it was time for the pair to breed again. As a result, the parents might actually forego breeding that year. To avoid this problem, the researchers decided to capture the chick that resulted from the second egg as well. This way, the parents would be free to breed again the following spring. This technique would actually triple the number of chicks that a pair could produce in one breeding cycle.

The disaster of 1985

As the captive-breeding program was becoming established and researchers continued to study condors in the wild, an event occurred that would once again bring turmoil to the condor recovery effort. During the winter of 1984–85, six of the remaining fifteen wild condors disappeared. This event was made even more significant by the fact that four of these birds were from different mating pairs, reducing the breeding population of condors from five pairs to only one.

Until this time, condor biologists had intended to leave a number of adult birds in the wild. It was thought that these adults would serve as mentors for juvenile birds that were released. Because they were familiar with foraging areas and nesting and roosting sites, these experienced birds would be able to teach the younger ones how to survive in the wild. However, faced with a total wild population of only nine birds, the condor recovery team proposed that all remaining birds be captured and brought into the breeding program. This decision, it argued, would ensure the survival of the remaining condors and enhance the success of the captive-breeding program.

This proposal instantly met with opposition from the same people who were initially critical of the recovery team's plan. Of foremost concern was that once condors were removed from the wild, no effort would be made to continue habitat protection measures. Even the National Audubon Society, which up until this point had been a supportive recovery team partner, criticized the capture plan.

It expressed concern that condors reared in zoos would be too familiar with people and might not survive when released back into the wild without the guidance of mentor birds. Audubon biologist Jesse Grantham feared that "we'll be ending a culture in the wild, and we won't be able to bring it back."[9] After the U.S. Fish and Wildlife Service decided to proceed, the National Audubon Society filed a lawsuit to halt the captures.

Meanwhile, the wild condor population continued to drop. In January 1986 an adult female was found ill and died shortly after being brought to the San Diego Wild Animal Park. Examination showed shotgun pellets imbedded throughout her body. This shooting incident, however, is not what killed her. Instead, her death was the result of a single bullet ingested while feeding on a carcass; like so many birds before her, she had died of lead poisoning.

By June 1986, with only five condors left in the wild, the courts ruled in favor of the U.S. Fish and Wildlife Service's plan to capture the remaining birds. At the same time, the service created two more wildlife refuges to provide additional habitat for condors once releases began in the future. The first refuge was the 1,800-acre Hopper Mountain National Wildlife Refuge, adjacent to the Sespe Condor Sanctuary. The second was the 13,500-acre Bitter Creek National Wildlife Refuge, a known condor foraging area. The service's securing of this additional condor habitat was an important step in proving its sincerity in continuing habitat preservation efforts.

The last wild condor

On Easter Sunday 1987, the last wild condor was captured, marking the end of the era of the free-flying condor in North America. He was identified as AC-9 (adult condor number 9), a seven-year-old adult male weighing nineteen pounds. AC-9 was captured at 10:15 A.M. by a net shot over him as he fed on the carcass of a calf. The condor team was pleased to have captured all of the remaining birds safely, but it was nevertheless a difficult moment.

Describing his feelings, Joe Dowhan, the coordinator of the condor recovery project said, "He [AC-9] was so hungry that he came to eat almost as soon as it was light, but we were ready. It was really very easy. But mind you, I have trouble talking about it even now. It was a bittersweet moment. We had to bring him in for his own good, but it was also sad, because he was the last one out there."[10] With the departure of AC-9, the skies above the continent were without the condor for the first time in over ten thousand years.

The last wild condor in North America was captured in 1987.

Even though this moment marked the end, at least temporarily, of condors in the wild, it also marked the beginning of what biologists hoped would be the eventual resurrection of the species. This hope depended on the twenty-seven condors then living at the Los Angeles Zoo and the San Diego Wild Animal Park. Would the condor breed in captivity? The future of the bird lay in the answer to this question.

4

The California Condor Captive-Breeding Progam

ALTHOUGH SMALL NUMBERS of California condors had been held in captivity since the 1900s, these birds were rarely housed together and no real attempt had been made to encourage their breeding. The National Zoo housed a group of condors together in the 1920s and reported egg-laying by a twelve-year-old bird. Eventually, though, it was discovered that all members of the group were female, shattering hopes that they would ever produce a chick. When condor recovery plans were first developed, only one California condor remained in captivity. This bird, named Topa Topa, had been found as an eleven-month-old near starvation in the wild in 1967. He had been housed alone since that time at the Los Angeles Zoo.

Critics of the condor recovery plan argued that the lack of experience raising condors in captivity would pose a significant challenge to the newly formed breeding effort. Biologists, however, were more confident. They planned to follow an existing successful condor-breeding model—that of the Andean condor.

Breeding Andean condors

Andean condors have been bred in captivity for over 150 years. The first success was in 1840, at the London Zoo. In 1942 the San Diego Zoo began a long-running breeding

Biologists learned more about how to save the California condor (pictured) using Andean condors to test different methods of breeding and raising chicks.

and rearing program for Andean condors. This program led to the discoveries that Andean condors will double-clutch if an egg is removed and that people could artificially raise chicks successfully.

When it became clear that any plan to save the California condor would involve a captive-breeding component, biologists began to make a more concentrated effort to learn as much as possible from Andean condors. Because the Andean condor's numbers were more secure, it was safe to use these birds to test different methods of breeding and raising chicks. Andean condor pairs were established at the San Diego Zoo, the San Diego Wild Animal Park, the Bronx Zoo, and the U.S. Fish and Wildlife Service's Patuxent Wildlife Research Center. From 1980 to 1987, biologists worked closely with these birds to learn all of the important details they hoped would benefit their efforts to breed the Andean condor's endangered cousin. They would soon have the opportunity to draw on what they had learned.

Condorminiums

The San Diego Wild Animal Park and the Los Angeles Zoo were the first facilities to receive permission to breed California condors in captivity. In 1992 a third facility, the Peregrine Fund's World Center for Birds of Prey in Boise, Idaho, was granted permission as well.

One of the first steps in the establishment of the breeding program was the construction of appropriate housing for the huge birds. The resulting enclosures, christened condorminiums, were specially designed with the condors' needs in mind. These enclosures are located out of public view in an attempt to keep the birds as isolated as possible. Although the enclosures vary slightly at each facility, they have certain features in common. The condorminiums consist of large individual pens, each with free-flight enclosures measuring twenty to forty feet high and eighty to one hundred feet long. They also contain roosting, bathing, and nesting areas and catch pens. Special perches in the flight cages are actually scales, allowing biologists to obtain a bird's weight when it lands.

Adjacent to the birds' enclosures are support buildings serving a variety of purposes. Each facility maintains special chambers for incubating eggs, rearing chicks, and housing very young condors. Additionally, all of the condors can be monitored without being disturbed through the use of special remote video cameras.

The World Center for Birds of Prey

Boise, Idaho, is home to the Peregrine Fund's World Center for Birds of Prey, a facility dedicated to education, research, and breeding of rare and endangered birds. The Peregrine Fund was instrumental in restoring Peregrine falcons in the United States, and in its twenty-five-year history it has released over four thousand birds of various species to the wild. Since 1993 the center has been home to the third captive-breeding colony of California condors and oversees the release of condors in Arizona. Besides the important work occurring behind the scenes here, visitors to the fund's interpretive center also have the opportunity to learn more about the birds through multimedia presentations and interactive displays. Additionally, the center exhibits fourteen raptor species, providing a rare opportunity to view these birds up close. The center was the first facility to have California condors on public display since the 1970s.

The condor population grows

The first condors to move into the newly established breeding center at the San Diego Wild Animal Park were a chick and an immature male, both captured in the wild in 1982. In 1983 two more chicks and four eggs joined the breeding program. The first of these eggs to hatch produced a chick, named Sisquoc, who was celebrated as the first California condor ever hatched in captivity. In 1984 eight eggs and one chick were brought into captivity. The removal of eggs and chicks from wild nesting condors continued until 1987, when no more pairs remained. The majority of collected eggs hatched successfully, causing the condor's population to grow for the first time in recorded history—from twenty-two birds in 1983 to twenty-seven birds in 1987.

Although hatching these collected eggs increased the condor population, the most important goal was getting the adult condors to produce eggs themselves in their new captive environment. When the breeding program first began, only three female condors were old enough to breed in the entire population. One of these, the one identified as UN-1, had already established a pair bond with the six-year-old male called AC-4. On March 3, 1988, the pair produced an egg. This egg hatched on April 29, revealing the first California condor not only hatched but also bred in captivity. This was an important milestone for the condor recovery effort, proving that condors could be successfully bred in zoos. The significance of this moment was reflected in the name chosen for this landmark chick. Condors hatched in captivity had all been given names taken from the Chumash tribe of Native Americans, who revered the birds. But the Chumash word for the condor itself, *molloko*, had never been used until then.

The captive-breeding program at the San Diego Wild Animal Park has increased the condor population.

From that point on, the population of condors grew rapidly. Each year, as new pairs formed and younger birds reached breeding age, the number of chicks hatching accelerated. By 1991 the condor population had soared to fifty-two captive birds. Biologists working to raise condors at the breeding facilities had found a way to nurture this critically endangered bird back from the brink of extinction. Their success was a result of technology, teamwork, and extraordinary human effort.

Hatching condors

When captive condor breeding began, the adult condors did very little of the work themselves. Instead, once the egg was laid, it was tended completely by zoo biologists in order to increase the odds that the chick would survive. Initially, people raised all of the eggs laid. Later, as condor numbers grew, biologists began leaving some of the eggs to be raised by the parent birds.

Eggs that are taken are placed in special incubators that carefully control the temperature and humidity. To best ensure hatching, the eggs are maintained between ninety-seven and ninety-eight degrees Fahrenheit. The incubator automatically turns each egg once every hour, just as the parent bird would do in the nest. Because the eggs actually lose weight through evaporation as the chick develops inside, each egg is weighed daily. By adjusting the humidity level, biologists can be sure the egg does not lose too much or too little weight. Biologists also monitor the developing chick by candling the egg each day. Candling is a procedure that shines a bright light through the shell of an egg to see the embryo inside. Candling is first performed to determine if the egg is fertile, or actually has a chick inside. After a few days of incubation, blood vessels can be seen within the egg, signaling the presence of a developing chick. Later, candling is useful for observing the changes taking place as the embryo grows.

Eventually, after fifty-four to fifty-eight days of incubation, the chick will "pip," or make the first hole in the shell in its attempt to hatch. The time between pipping and

health problems due to the interbreeding of close relatives, a process known as inbreeding. Therefore, it is vital that biologists understand the family relationships between the birds in their care so that close relatives will not be bred together. A special test, known as DNA fingerprinting, was performed on blood taken from each of the twenty-seven

Hand puppets that look exactly like adult condors are used to feed condor chicks in captive-breeding programs.

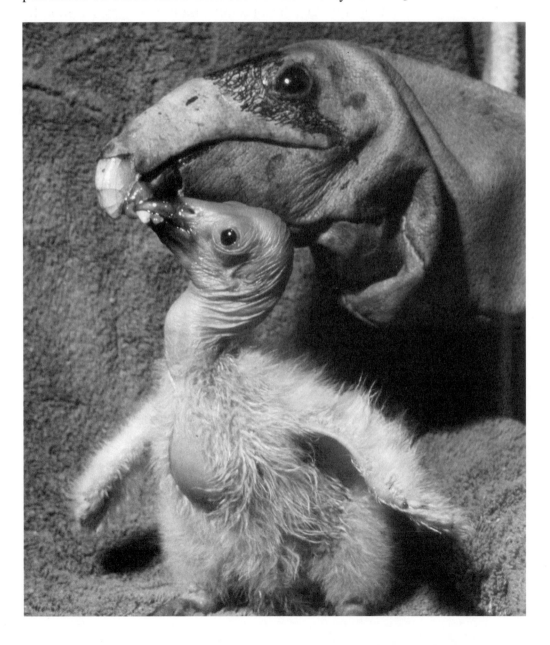

condors that started the breeding program. The results showed that these condors contained fourteen different "founder" birds, representing three lines, or clans. This information was entered into a computer that is used to determine the best pairings from a genetic standpoint. This will allow the condor recovery team to maintain the highest level of genetic diversity possible.

Ready for release

The issue of genetic diversity was also an important consideration as the team tried to determine when it should begin releasing condors into the wild. In October 1986 the team set several conditions that would need to be met before condors could be set free. The first condition was that 96 percent of the founder birds' genes had to be represented in the captive population. Second, there needed to be at least three breeding pairs of condors providing young for release. And third, captive breeding had

 Genetic Bottleneck

Despite the safeguards to minimize inbreeding among condor pairs in captive-breeding programs, the low numbers of birds used to establish these programs may result in a variety of problems in the future. Animals like the condor, which have experienced a severe reduction in numbers, are said to have suffered a "genetic bottleneck." These animals declined to near extinction (maybe as a result of disease or natural disaster) and then rebuilt their population from the small number of individual animals that remained. This type of inbreeding is known to lead to physical and behavioral defects such as low reproductive rates, poor disease resistance, physical deformities, and problems with social interactions.

Biologists admit that the California condor is currently experiencing a genetic bottleneck. Although effects of inbreeding have not been seen so far, it may take several generations for them to become apparent.

to have become consistent enough that there would be birds available for release every year. As the breeding season ended in 1991, it appeared that these conditions could be met. Condors were breeding well and the time had come to see if captive-bred condors would give their species a second chance at survival in the wild.

5

Return to the Wild

BEFORE THE CAPTIVE breeding of California condors had even begun, the condor recovery team anticipated the future release of birds into the wild. In preparation for that day, it once again turned to the Andean condor to help develop the methods that would make the release program successful. The team members began by releasing eleven captive-bred Andean condors in Peru between 1980 and 1984. Through this research, biologists learned how to care for and monitor the newly released birds. They were also able to observe how well these birds adjusted to life in the wild. However, concerned about differences in the climate, landscape, and levels of human activity between Peru and the proposed release site in California, the team planned a second release of Andean condors, this time in the Los Padres National Forest.

To eliminate the possibility that Andean condors introduced to California would become permanently established there, the team decided to release only female birds. Between 1988 and 1991, thirteen Andean condors were released. These condors were taken as chicks to the release sites, where they grew up in netted enclosures built on cliff faces. When they reached fledging age, the nets were removed and the condors could come and go as they pleased. The team provided carcasses for the released birds to feed on, just as they planned to do with newly released California condors.

Of the thirteen condors released, one died after colliding with power lines and two others failed to adjust to the wild and were recaptured. The ten remaining birds, however, were successful at living in the wild and traveled long distances, even finding food on their own. Michael Wallace of the Los Angeles Zoo shared the feeling of triumph felt by the team: "We took condors from start to finish to see if we could put them in the field. We showed we knew what we were doing and that we could learn to do it even better."[12] At the end of the release experiment, all of the Andean condors were recaptured and eventually released in Peru.

The first release

After the successful experiment with the Andeans, the team was ready to proceed with releasing California condors. By 1991 fifty-two birds were in captivity, including nine breeding pairs. Two chicks, a female named Xewe (pronounced Gay-wee) and a male named Chocuyens (Cho-koo-yenz), were selected to be the first condors set free. These individuals were chosen, in part, because they

Released condors feed on a carcass provided for them by a team of researchers.

were technically expendable. Although the loss of any bird would be significant, these chicks had numerous relatives in the captive population. Therefore, if they died, their genes would still be well represented.

Originally, the team hoped to release three condors together, but no other chick was considered genetically suitable that year. Instead, the team decided to release the two California condors with two Andean condors to create a suitable group. Forming a group like this would more closely imitate the natural social structure of the condors and would subject them to less stress. The four birds were very close in age and had been raised together most of their lives. Additionally, all of the chicks had been raised in strict isolation from people. They had been fed by puppets and monitored by video camera, never having seen a single human.

To give these birds the best chance at making a successful transition to the wild, the biologists gave careful consideration to choosing the release site. First, the site needed to be as isolated as possible to minimize the human contact the condors would face. Second, the site should be as free as possible from obstacles that might pose a hazard to condors learning to fly, such as power lines and oil wells. Third, the site must be able to provide suitable flying conditions as well as protection for the young birds. For example, a location along a cliff face would safeguard the chicks and provide a perch from which to learn to fly along the rising air currents. Finally, the site must be contained in one of the areas previously set aside for condors, in their traditional range area. Meeting these requirements would ensure the young condors the highest level of protection from people.

After considering all of the possible release locations, the team decided on a site called the Arundell Cliffs, located in the Sespe Condor Sanctuary in Ventura, California. A release pen, designed to simulate a small cave similar to the ones in which condors typically nest, was constructed out of metal, wood, foam, and cement. It was then lifted by helicopter onto the selected cliff ledge.

In October 1991 the four Andean and California condor chicks were transferred from the Los Angeles Zoo to the release site. They were housed in the pen until January 14, 1992, when the team opened the door and set them free. At first, the birds were timid, only exploring the cliff and flapping their wings. Only one of the Andeans took a short flight that day. The next day, however, Xewe took flight, and within a few weeks, all of the birds were flying short distances to explore the surrounding area.

The first few months after release are considered the most dangerous for the condors as they adjust to their new life. During this time the biologists anxiously monitor their progress to see how they respond to the people and obstacles they encounter. All of the condors released are fitted with two radio transmitters—one on the wing and one on the tail. These transmitters allow biologists to track the movements of the condors, even when they cannot see them. Each bird also wears a color-coded number on its wing for identification.

Things seemed to be going well for the newly released condors. They were becoming bolder in their explorations, flying up to twenty miles in all directions from their cliff home. It was, however, during one of these flights that a condor had its first negative interaction with a person. In July, Xewe was seen being shot at by two men with rifles. Fortunately she was unharmed. One of the men was captured, eventually convicted, and fined fifteen hundred dollars. As a result, the Forest Service began an intensive hunter education program in the area. Despite this incident, it was clear that, so far, the young condors were succeeding in their new life in the wild. Because they were doing so well, the team decided to replace the Andean condors with a new group of California condor chicks. The Andean condors were captured in September 1992 and were re-released in South America.

The first setbacks

Soon after Xewe and Chocuyens were left on their own, the condor release program was dealt its first blow.

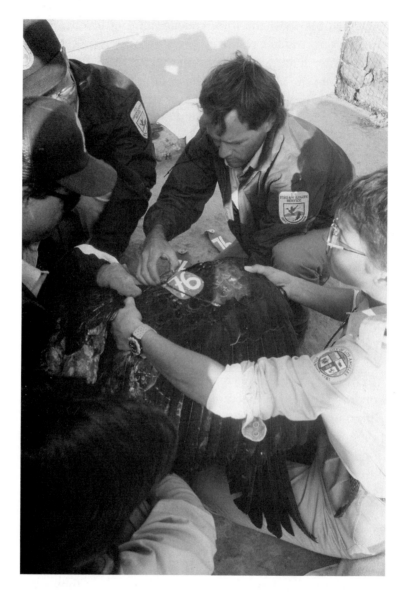

Chocuyens was found dead on October 8, after ingesting ethylene glycol, a toxic ingredient of antifreeze. This loss was especially troubling because it was the first time any condor had ever died in this manner, thus expanding the list of hazards the birds faced. Team members had anticipated some setbacks like this, so although they were disappointed, they remained confident the release program would succeed.

On December 1, 1992, six more captive-bred condors were released to join Xewe in the Sespe Condor Sanctuary. These birds quickly formed a strong social unit and appeared to be adjusting well.

One of the most important tasks the team performed following the new release was providing the birds with appropriate food sources. Because, in the past, so many condors had died from poisoning after eating carcasses containing lead shot, it was important to minimize the possibility of this happening again. It also takes a long time before young condors build up enough strength to be able to travel the long distances required to find food on their own. Thus, while these condors were becoming familiar with their new environment, the team placed carcasses of livestock and road-killed animals out for the birds. The food was strategically positioned in areas away from human activity in the hope that the condors would learn to seek food in similar locations.

Keeping the condors away from areas where humans were active was turning out to be a major challenge. Because condors are scavengers, they are naturally curious birds and are attracted to areas of activity. Biologists were concerned that the birds seemed drawn to one area in particular, Pyramid Lake, where there were lots of people and

 ## Monitoring Released Condors

Because of the continued risk that condors face from exposure to toxins in their environment, biologists closely monitor the birds' health after release. Occasionally biologists will bait traps with calf carcasses in an effort to capture condors for physical examinations. These exams are an opportunity to evaluate the overall health of the birds, weigh them, and draw blood samples. These blood samples are later analyzed for the presence of disease or toxins. During the exams, the condors are also fitted with new radio transmitters and identification tags on their wings so that they can be watched closely once re-released.

obstacles. This is where Chocuyens had eaten the antifreeze that killed him. Condors began appearing frequently in this area and could be seen walking on roads, landing in yards, and even taking food from picnickers. The tameness shown by the condors surprised biologists, who thought it would have been prevented by raising the birds in isolation.

Even more troubling was the tendency of the condors to use power poles as perches. This was dangerous for two reasons. First, as condors flew near the power lines, it was likely that a collision would occur. Also, because the condor's wings are so long, as the birds come in for a landing on a pole, their wingtips can easily touch the lines, resulting in electrocution. This concern proved to be well founded when three condors were killed in power-line incidents between May and October 1993. As a result, the decision was made to select a new release site that was even more isolated.

This new site was in Lion Canyon, a remote area of the Los Padres National Forest. The four condors remaining in the wild were captured and transferred to this location, where they were joined by five more chicks in December 1993. The older birds were released one at a time over a period of several weeks in the hope that they would not return to their old home. Unfortunately, three condors returned to their original release site and resumed their habitats of perching on power poles and hanging around humans. Worried that the newly released younger birds would copy this behavior, the team captured the offending condors and returned them to the captive-breeding program. Shortly thereafter, one of the five newly released birds was killed by a collision with a power line in a completely different area. Another young bird was seen frequenting the same area and was therefore captured before it, too, had an accident.

Aversion training

Obviously, something needed to be done about the power-line problem. The team decided to begin a new, cre-

Biologists use aversion training to teach condors to shun power poles and other human obstacles.

ative program to train the birds to fear power poles. This program, called aversion training, was designed to teach condors to stay away from power poles and other human obstacles. The flight pens at the captive-breeding facilities were refitted to include mock power poles. These poles were rigged to deliver a mild six-volt shock to any condor landing on them.

Additionally, the team decided to solve the problem of the released condors being too tame by giving them negative associations with people. They realized that raising the condors in isolation was not enough; the birds needed to fear humans, not just be unfamiliar with them. To achieve this goal, young captive condors were purposely harassed every time they encountered people. When cleaning pens or capturing birds for exams, biologists were as loud and threatening as possible. They entered the cages yelling and waving their arms in an effort to frighten the condors. This experience was designed to give the condors a memory of humans as being scary creatures to avoid in the future. Both types of aversion training are still in use and have proven effective, for the most part, at keeping released condors safer.

In fact, in 1995 fourteen young condors were released in Lion Canyon, all of which had undergone aversion training prior to release. The results of the training were significant. None of the birds were seen landing on power poles, and they mostly avoided areas of human activity. Only one condor showed curiosity toward people; it landed in a campground and begged for food from campers. This condor was captured and returned to captivity.

Parent-reared chicks

Although aversion training had helped condors gain a fear of people, biologists wondered whether they could do more to ensure that released chicks would be successful in the wild. One of their biggest concerns was the lack of guidance the chicks received from older birds. However, by 1995 the captive condors were breeding so well that biologists decided to try a new experiment. Four of the chicks hatched that year were left to be raised by their parents. After three months with their parents, the chicks were moved to a specially designed rearing facility at the Hopper Mountain National Wildlife Refuge. There they were placed in artificial nest caves with adjoining flight cages. It was hoped that placing chicks in a more natural environment would better adjust them to life in the wild.

In February 1996 these parent-reared condors were released at a newly developed site called Castle Crags, located in the Los Padres National Forest. Soon after, older

birds from the nearby Lion Canyon release site arrived and began interacting with the juveniles. This interaction was encouraging to biologists, who hoped that the young birds could learn from those with more experience. Having older birds to serve as mentors, or teachers, closely follows how condor chicks would naturally learn. In fact, as releases have continued in following years, this mentoring has also continued. The chicks that receive this mentoring demonstrate a better ability to socialize appropriately with other condors.

Biologists are encouraged by the interaction they have witnessed among released condors.

Grand Canyon condors

As condor numbers continued to grow in southern California, plans were made to develop a completely separate area to establish another population. After considering many proposals, the condor recovery team selected the Vermilion Cliffs in Arizona, located approximately fifty miles north of the Grand Canyon. Once plans to release condors in this area were announced, however, they were greeted with mixed reactions. In what became an emotionally charged public debate, landowners and elected officials confronted environmentalists and condor recovery team members with their concerns. Many residents of Arizona and Utah, the area where the new population would range, feared that the arrival of the condors would bring new government regulations and restrictions on the use of their land.

Many elected officials thought these fears were warranted. They had seen other programs to revive endangered

 Notes from the Field—Grand Canyon Area

The Peregrine Fund monitors condors released in Arizona and provides updates on their activities on its website. Here, biologist Shawn Farry provides an account of the disappearance of a young condor in February 2000 near the Grand Canyon:

Despite their size, life in the wild holds risks for condors, especially young inexperienced individuals. This week we were again reminded of these risks with the unfortunate mortality of a second young bird at the Hurricane Cliffs' release site. The carcass of Condor 97 was located at the base of the Hurricane fault six miles south of the Hurricane release box on 2/4/00. Condor 97 had no history of health or behavioral problems that foreshadowed this mortality. Upon release Condor 97 weighed 18 lb. and upon recovery the carcass weighed 17 lb. and appeared in good overall physical condition. Portions of the carcass had been plucked and the right leg and breast had been fed on extensively. What we assume to be eagle whitewash was prevalent in the area and on the carcass. In addition, there appeared to be a single talon puncture under the left eye. Preliminary examination of the carcass pointed to a golden eagle as the cause of death. In January 1997 Condor 42 was killed by a golden eagle under very similar circumstances.

species result in lost development opportunities and in unwanted restrictions. Many people in the area already regarded the endangered desert tortoise, spotted owl, and prairie dog as villains due to provisions in place to protect them. "There was already a feeling of very great and intense distrust of and almost anger at the Endangered Species Act in Washington County," said Robert Dibblee, an aide to Senator Orrin Hatch of Utah. "We need to protect species, but should be able to take into account the economy."[13] Utah residents Janice and Larry Esplin shared their views of condors with the U.S. Fish and Wildlife Service. "The condor is not a majestic bird but a common buzzard which lives on road kill," they wrote. "If you think that we or any tourist would be excited to see these birds gnawing away on a dead animal carcass along the road you are very mistaken."[14]

Biologists for the condor program were surprised to receive such negative, and sometimes hostile, reactions to a bird almost universally beloved by Californians. "It's been really frustrating," said Tom Robinson, director of conservation policy for the Grand Canyon Trust. "If ever there was a slam-dunk issue, this should have been it. Here's a bird that has no potential impact on any industry, any business, anybody."[15]

After receiving input from politicians and the public, the U.S. Fish and Wildlife Service developed an agreement about the condors' release. The condors at the Vermilion Cliffs would be designated as a nonessential experimental population under the Endangered Species Act. That meant that the presence of the condors would not restrict current land uses or activities such as agriculture, mining, livestock grazing, or sport hunting. Biologists hoped that once the condors were released, people would realize that they posed no threat.

In December 1996 six young condors were released on the Vermilion Cliffs. For the first time in over seventy years, condors once again flew over the Grand Canyon. Another release site, Hurricane Cliffs, was later established nearby. As with the reintroductions in southern California, the

Due to condor releases on Vermilion Cliffs, condors are now flying over the Grand Canyon for the first time in over seventy years.

newly released Arizona condors occasionally encountered difficulties. Two were killed by golden eagles, and one died from a power-line collision. A few others have demonstrated characteristic condor curiosity by approaching hikers and homes. Three condors even took a stroll into a park nature center, much to the surprise of visitors. Most, however, are finding food and socializing normally, signaling a successful transition to life in the wild.

The Ventana wilderness release

Because of the success of the Arizona and southern California condor populations, biologists were encouraged to establish a third group. The chosen location was the Ventana Wilderness Sanctuary, located along the rugged Big Sur coast of central California. Four chicks were released in January 1997, but they soon got into trouble. This group of puppet-raised chicks demonstrated extreme friendliness toward people. They approached hikers and landed on the roofs of homes in the area. Fearing for their safety, the team captured them and returned them to the Los Angeles Zoo.

The team tried again in September, this time using chicks raised by adult condors. The chicks were put in a

 Notes from the Field—Big Sur
Biologists from the Ventana Wilderness Society monitor the activity of condors in the Big Sur release site area on California's central coast. On the society's website, these researchers share important milestones in the condors' new lives in the wild:

February 1999: The biggest impact upon the young condors this month was the return of the older condors to the release site. The older condors immediately took the upper hand, chasing the younger condors away from the carcasses. After the older condors grew tired of dominating the younger ones, and had amply fed, they began to warm up to the new birds. As the month wore on the older and younger condors began to preen one another and even started roosting together in the same trees.

March 1999: Y68 set out on a journey that took him around the entire northern half of the Ventana Wilderness Area, a flight of approximately 120 miles. We have reason to believe that Y68 may have fed on the carcass of a large range cow while traveling on his 18-day long sortie.

November 1999: B71 was observed feeding at Sea Lion Cove on a marine mammal carcass. Y94, following the lead of her turkey vulture companions, discovered two carcasses: a cattle carcass on a Big Sur ranch, and a marine mammal carcass at Sea Lion Cove. This "natural foraging" behavior is a good sign of maturity. The maturity of the young, free-flying birds has also been demonstrated by their recent improvement in defending carcasses from golden eagles.

large flight pen, where they could develop flying skills before they were released. Accompanying them in the flight pen was an adult condor that would not be released. Instead, the adult bird would provide important mentoring to the chicks, teaching them how to socialize properly. This new tactic was successful. When released, these chicks avoided people and formed relationships with other condors. This technique of housing chicks with adults prior to release has now become standard.

This adaptability by team members has been key to the success of the recovery of the California condor. When faced with obstacles and failures, they refine their techniques until they are successful. Without the team's dedication and willingness to learn, the condor might have joined the ever-growing list of creatures now gone from our world.

6

The Future of the Condor

WITHOUT QUESTION, THE successes of the California condor recovery program have been substantial. Condors are breeding consistently in captivity, and many of their offspring have been released to experience life in the wild. The numbers strikingly illustrate the dramatic increase: from a low of twenty-two birds in 1983 to one hundred and sixty-nine birds in October 2000. Of these, one hundred and thirty-three are in captivity and thirty-six are in the wild.

Downlisting the condor

As these numbers increase, biologists can begin to look toward the condor's future. The ultimate goal of the recovery program is the "downlisting" of the species under the Endangered Species Act. Downlisting means that the California condor would no longer be considered endangered and would instead be classified as threatened. Although condors would still be monitored and protected, downlisting would signify that their numbers were secure.

Before the captive-breeding and release efforts had begun, the condor recovery team had developed very specific objectives that needed to be met in order to downlist the condor. First, there would have to be at least two completely separate wild populations numbering at least 150 birds. Having more than one population is extremely important, especially for an animal of such low numbers. A

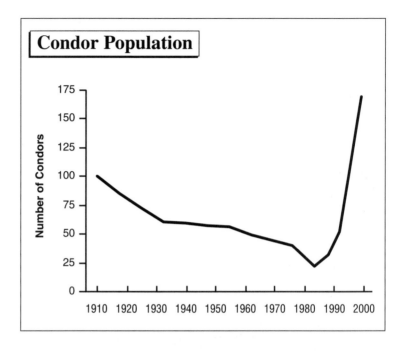

Condor Population

single small population would be at great risk of being wiped out if a disease epidemic or natural disaster struck. Thus, additional populations serve as an insurance policy against extinction. Second, each population must be growing and have at least fifteen breeding pairs among its members. Third, each population must contain descendants from some of the original founder birds to ensure the greatest genetic diversity possible.

As the Grand Canyon and California condor populations begin to grow, other release sites are now being considered. The Ventana Wilderness Society, managers of the Big Sur release site, are investigating the possibility of bringing condors further inland, to California's Diablo Mountains and the Sierra Nevada, both part of the condor's historic range. Biologists are also interested in releasing condors along Mexico's Baja Peninsula, where plentiful food is available in the form of marine mammals and fish.

Socializing

The optimism that biologists feel for the condor's future in the wild is mainly due to the fact that released condors are more frequently observed actually acting like condors. These pioneering birds are forming natural social groups and, for the most part, adjusting well. In the early days of the release program, young condors did not seem to know how to behave properly around humans or other condors. But now that the team is allowing parent condors to raise their chicks and is providing mentoring opportunities for them upon release, juveniles are behaving much more appropriately. In fact, condor observers now routinely see older birds teaching chicks and integrating them into their dominance hierarchies.

In 1996 two groups of condors released thirty-five miles apart in Los Padres National Forest began mingling for the first time. They began roosting as a flock, preening one another, and even made some foraging trips together, finding a naturally occurring carcass. This activity was a huge

---

The Condor Recovery Program Goes Full Circle: AC-8 Returns to the Wild

In 1986 the last wild female condor was captured in the Los Padres National Forest. This bird, known as AC-8 (adult condor number 8), was brought to the San Diego Wild Animal Park to join the newly developed captive-breeding program. AC-8 is considered a "founder" bird of the captive-breeding population and is one of the oldest condors alive. Her age is unknown, but it is estimated to be nearly forty years. Over fourteen years, AC-8 produced nine offspring. Many of her chicks have gone on to produce offspring of their own.

Having passed breeding age, her contribution to the program was celebrated when, in April 2000, she was the first of the original wild-caught birds to be released into her former territory in the Sespe Condor Sanctuary. Accompanying AC-8 were two ten-month-old captive-bred condors. Biologists hoped that AC-8 would serve as a mentor to these younger birds and others already released, guiding them to a successful life in the wild.

Released condors are forming natural social groups, which are crucial for their survival.

breakthrough for a program that had originally been plagued by setbacks due to the birds' lack of social skills.

One of the most exciting social events occurred in April 1999 when Ventana Wilderness Society biologists observed the arrival of condor Y30 at the Big Sur release site. Y30 was one of twenty-two condors released in southern California at a site in Los Padres National Forest. None of the southern California condors had traveled that far north before. Her arrival seemed to spark an interest in travel for the Big Sur condors, some of which flew as far as 125 miles south, into the range of the southern California birds. Biologists had long anticipated the moment when the two California groups would meet. They hope that, as their numbers grow and the birds gain more experience, these groups will merge to form one population ranging throughout the wilderness along the California coast.

The Arizona condors are beginning to travel more widely as well. In 1999 condor number 19 disappeared from her release area, flying out of range of her radio transmitter. Biologists feared she was lost until, twelve days later, she was spotted in southwestern Wyoming, 310 miles away. Then, demonstrating the condor's remarkable ability to quickly fly long distances, she returned home to the Vermilion Cliffs in only two days, following a historic condor route along the Colorado River. After her trip, three other birds journeyed a distance of 500 miles, traveling to Colorado and back.

Some threats continue

Despite all of these successes, the condor's future in the wild will likely still be in question for some time. Many of the threats that helped bring about the condor's original decline still exist. Education and public relations efforts have

 Andean Condor Conservation in Venezuela

The future is looking a bit brighter for Andean condors. Considered extinct in Venezuela since the 1900s, condors are now being released there through a program supported by the Cleveland Zoological Society. The first condors released were chicks raised by California condors as part of the "parenting lessons" they received when the California condor recovery program first began. Now, additional Andean condors from a number of zoo breeding programs are being returned to the wild in South America. In addition to releasing birds, the recovery team is concentrating on establishing a conservation education program in the surrounding area. Because the condor is such a high-profile animal, the team hopes to use it as a tool to encourage the Venezuelan people to become interested in ecology and conservation. In an interview with the author, Stan Searles, curator of birds at the Cleveland Metroparks Zoo, explained: "Turning them [condors] loose is the easy part. We realize the project will only be successful if people are educated."

greatly increased awareness of the condor's plight, but isolated events of persecution by people continue. Two released condors, one in California and one in Arizona, have been shot and killed. The Arizona shooter was caught and prosecuted, receiving a fine of thirty-two hundred dollars. Because some people in the Grand Canyon area still resent

Despite the success of captive-breeding programs, condors are still plagued by threats such as hunters and toxins.

Stars of the Endangered Species Act

Certain animals, such as wolves, black-footed ferrets, and California condors, receive much more conservation money and attention than other rare species in the United States. Why do these creatures merit so much interest when other critically endangered species go virtually unnoticed? The answer is easy: for endangered species, charisma counts. The condor's large size, dramatic appearance, and compelling story make it the perfect public relations vehicle for media attention and fundraising. This star appeal, combined with its extremely low numbers, has transformed the condor into the poster child for the recovery of endangered species. But all of the attention given to endangered stars like the condor comes at a great cost to other less flashy plants and animals that continue to slip unnoticed ever further toward extinction. With intervention, the prospects of saving many of these species are great. But without the necessary public and government support, these less glamorous species will remain in the shadows of the superstars.

the presence of the condor, these troubling incidents may be repeated.

Of greater concern to biologists, however, are the ongoing threats of toxins, primarily lead, present in the environment that could endanger the health or lives of the condors. In a report for the journal *Conservation Biology*, Vicky Meretsky and her colleagues analyzed the effect that lead poisoning is having on the condor population. Their study found that thirteen released birds have already tested positive for lead exposure or have become sickened by lead poisoning. All of these birds were recaptured for treatment and survived.

Meretsky, however, finds this sort of intervention impractical in the long run. "If lead contamination persists in the environment and increased feeding on natural carcasses continues, the ultimate mortality rates of released birds

Condor Ridge

Although condors have lived at the San Diego Wild Animal Park since 1982, they had not been on public display until the opening of the new Condor Ridge exhibit in 2000. The exhibit features five California condors and other rare wildlife of western North America. The six-story condor aviary is designed to mimic the birds' natural habitat by containing huge boulders and steep cliffs. Visitors to the observation deck can have an up-close view of condors interacting with one another, sunbathing, and flying. In an article in the May 25, 2000 *San Diego Union-Tribune*, Kim Peterson explains that, for park staff, Condor Ridge is a long-awaited chance to communicate the story of their work with the public. "We've done all this work behind the scenes and now we have an opportunity to share with people what this conservation program is all about," says Michael Mace, curator of birds at the park.

seem likely to converge on the unsustainably high rates of the historic wild population."[16] She is concerned that techniques used to teach the condors to become self-sufficient in finding food are actually causing the problem. Carcasses are left for condors in ever-changing locations to teach the birds how to forage naturally. This technique has been so successful that condors are frequently finding food on their own—often deer that have been killed by lead bullets.

Meretsky offers two possible solutions to the ongoing lead problem. One is to expand the size and number of condor reserves, where hunting would be forbidden. This solution is likely unfeasible due to the huge expense of purchasing land and the far-ranging habits of the condors. The second solution is more realistic: the use of nontoxic ammunition. These bullets are made from TTB ammunition material, a combination of tungsten, tin, and bismuth. This material has been proven to be nontoxic when fed to turkey vultures during research. Although TTB ammunition costs more, it compares favorably to lead in accuracy, range, and power—important considerations to hunters. Lead poisoning is considered such a serious threat, capable of jeopardizing the condor's future, that Meretsky sums up her report this way: "Because alternative nontoxic ammunitions appear to offer a long-term solution to lead poisoning at low cost, their adoption should become the overriding near-term goal of condor conservation efforts."[17]

Breeding in the wild

Although great concern should be given to the physical threats still facing condors, a more fundamental question remains: Will condors breed successfully in the wild? All recovery efforts will be useless unless condors can eventually sustain their own population. Reintroduced birds are just now approaching breeding age, and some initial courtship behaviors have already been observed. Breeding and laying eggs, however, are only the first steps. Biologists are concerned that the increasing presence of egg and nestling predators may hinder the condor's breeding success. Ravens are major predators of eggs, and their numbers are climbing throughout the West. In fact, ravens are known to have been the primary reason for breeding failure in historic condor populations. Because condors can do little to protect their eggs from ravens, this problem may require additional human assistance.

A further threat faced by nestlings is the abundance of golden eagles in condor country. Historically, condors nested in areas with few golden eagles. Today, however, eagles are common near release sites. The newly released condors, having no experience with eagles, may choose to nest close to their release site instead of moving to areas with fewer eagles. Golden eagles have already demonstrated the danger they pose to juveniles, having killed two newly released birds in Arizona. Nestlings will be even more vulnerable.

The fact that released condors must still contend with the same problems that drove them to near extinction is a source of extreme frustration for opponents of the condor recovery program. They argue that the environment is no

Golden eagles killed two newly released condors in Arizona.

longer fit for condors and that more effort should be directed toward improving the environment, not trying to "improve" condors by training them and manipulating their behavior to keep them safe. According to Mark Palmer, program director for the Earth Island Institute, an environmental organization opposed to the captive-breeding and release program:

We're just putting condors back into the wild environment where they don't survive without fixing what was wrong in the environment. The environmental hazards that caused the problem in the first place are still there. Throwing out condors into the wild, feeding them, these are artificial measures to maintain the bird; it's a zoo without bars. They went extinct for a reason in Arizona and putting them back there doesn't make a whole lot of sense.[18]

A question of cost?

Critics of the condor program also point to the enormous cost of recovery. So far, nearly $20 million has been spent, up to $35,000 per bird, making the condor program the costliest yet for saving an endangered species. The cost to achieve downlisting could pass $50 million. This money comes from a variety of sources. The federal government provides about $500,000 of the $1.7 million needed each year, with zoos and private nonprofit groups contributing the rest.

While some opponents to condor recovery dwell on cost, others raise more fundamental questions about how the United States views and manages endangered species. In his opinion piece written for *Discover* magazine in 1986, Bill Gilbert raises some thoughtful points. He observes that, although, in the eyes of science all endangered species are equally important, certain species—such as condors—are treated as "more equal" and receive the lion's share of resources and publicity. However, these "star animals" are often the ones that have the worst prospects for being saved and fill a fairly insignificant role in the environment. In fact, Gilbert believes the loss of a species like the condor might serve as a wake-up call to the public, ultimately doing more good than the struggle to save it. Writing about the possible extinction of the condor and the black-footed ferret, Gilbert argues,

This might not be such a terrible thing as is commonly, reflexively thought. The passing of two such celebrated species would dramatically call attention to the process of extinction, and the ways our activities now influence the process. Also, if the condor and ferret were to go we might be more greatly

Watching Wild Condors

Despite the condor's rarity, it is possible for people with patience and determination to catch a glimpse of one in the wild. The U.S. Fish and Wildlife Service maintains several observation areas near condor release sites. Two of these locations, Lion Canyon and Castle Crags, are in the Los Padres National Forest in southern California. Some observation sites are accessible only by hiking, bicycling, or horseback riding, but others can be reached by car (four-wheel drive recommended) when the weather is good. In Arizona, condors can frequently be seen from a viewing area below the Vermilion Cliffs. This site has attracted bird-watchers from around the world, eager to catch a glimpse of the extraordinary condor. However, condors can range hundreds of miles, so making a trip to a viewing area is no guarantee of sighting a condor! The U.S. Fish and Wildlife Service can provide directions to the best viewing spots.

At Lion Canyon and Castle Crags, bird-watchers may catch a rare glimpse of the condor.

motivated on behalf of other species that are headed in that direction.[19]

Questions of cost and the value of the recovery program ruffle the feathers of condor biologists. Lloyd Kiff of the Peregrine Fund responds:

> It pains me to hear the condor recovery program painted as a waste of money. On an international or even national scale, the amount of money spent on condors is comparatively negligible. We live in an affluent society where individual actors make greater sums in a year, and individual paintings sell for more at auction. Is not the condor worth an equivalent amount as an art form or for its entertainment value?[20]

Robert Mesta, coordinator for the condor recovery program, agrees: "It's an expensive proposition, but you couldn't buy one stealth bomber for that. If you divide the price by the number of birds, it's a lot, but if you look at what it costs each taxpayer, it's almost nothing."[21] Mesta also defends the expense of the program on a moral level:

> Doing what's right for these birds involves . . . accepting responsibility for our own actions. It comes from the philosophy that if you cause a problem, it's your responsibility to address it and fix it. Within our culture today this is the standard by which we measure our worth as a society. I believe this attitude translates over to our environment, too.[22]

A conservation symbol

A lot of people, including ordinary citizens, agree with Mesta. In California, the condor recovery effort has been extensively publicized, with every new batch of chicks a cause for rejoicing. This bald bird from prehistoric times has become an unlikely hero and a celebrated symbol for endangered species protection. Once teetering on the absolute edge of extinction, the condor now has a second chance. Perhaps more importantly, humans, too, now have a second chance to provide a safe world for condors. Only the future will tell if condors and humans succeed.

Notes

Chapter 1: Meet the Condor

1. Dick Smith, *Condor Journal*. Santa Barbara, CA: Capra, 1978, p. 102

Chapter 2: The Decline of the Condor

2. Quoted in Smith, *Condor Journal*, p. 87.
3. Quoted in Smith, *Condor Journal*, p. 89.
4. U.S. Fish and Wildlife Service, *California Condor Recovery Plan* (pamphlet), 3rd rev. Portland, OR: 1996, p. 11.
5. Quoted in P. J. S. Olney, G. M. Mace, and A. T. C. Feistner, eds., *Creative Conservation: Interactive Management of Wild and Captive Animals*. London: Chapman and Hall, 1994, p. 412.
6. Quoted in Wayne Grady, *Vultures: Nature's Ghastly Gourmet*. Vancouver: Greystone Books, 1997, p. 71.

Chapter 3: The California Condor Recovery Program

7. Carl Koford, *The California Condor*. New York: Dover Publications, 1952, p. 135.
8. Quoted in Grady, *Vultures*, p. 74.
9. Quoted in Jamie Murphy, "Last Days of the Condor? North America's Biggest Land Bird in Trouble," *Time*, December 30, 1985, p. 68.
10. Quoted in Christopher Lewis, "Endangered and Embroiled: Controversy Continues to Beset Attempts to Save the Condor," *Sports Illustrated*, October 31, 1988, p. 84.

Chapter 4: The California Condor Captive-Breeding Program

11. San Diego Zoo, Center for the Reproduction of Endangered Species, "Hatching" (fact sheet), 2000. www.sandiegozoo.org/cres/hatching.html.

Chapter 5: Return to the Wild

12. Quoted in Jeffrey P. Cohn, "The Flight of the California Condor: After More than a Decade of Captive Breeding, the Big Bird Is on a Trajectory Toward Recovery," *Bioscience*, April 1993, p. 206+.

13. Quoted in Mary R. Pols, "Condor Conundrum: Plan to Reintroduce Endangered California Bird to Grand Canyon Area Angers Residents of Region, but a Compromise Is Reached," *Los Angeles Times*, April 28, 1996, p. 3+.

14. Quoted in Pols, "Condor Conundrum," p. 3+.

15. Quoted in Tom Kenworthy, "Wary Arizonans Give California Condors a Chilly Reception," *Seattle Times*, August 18, 1996, p. A16.

Chapter 6: The Future of the Condor

16. Vicky Meretsky et al., "Demography of the California Condor: Implications for Reestablishment," *Conservation Biology*, August 2000, p. 963.

17. Meretsky et al., "Demography of the California Condor," p. 966.

18. Quoted in Michael Ybarra, "Is This Bird Worth $20 Million?" *Los Angeles Times*, September 14, 1997.

19. Bill Gilbert, "Why Don't We Pull the Plug on the Condor and Ferret? *Discover*, July 1986, p. 81

20. Quoted in Todd Wilkinson, "Homecoming," *National Parks*, May/June 1996, p. 40.

21. Quoted in Ybarra, "Is this bird worth $20 million?"

22. Wilkinson, "Homecoming," p. 40+.

Glossary

aversion training: Teaching condors to fear people or objects that could cause them harm.

breakout: The process of providing human assistance to a condor chick hatching from an egg.

brood: The act of a parent bird covering its chicks to warm them on the nest.

candling: The process of shining a bright, concentrated light through an egg to observe the development of the embryo inside.

carrion: The dead and decaying flesh of an animal.

caruncle: The fleshy crest on the head of a male Andean condor.

Cathartidae: The family of vultures, including the condor, with representatives living in North and South America.

census: A counting of a certain population of animals or plants.

Ciconiiformes: The order of birds made up of the herons, storks, and Cathartid (North and South American) vultures.

clutch: The set of eggs produced in one normal laying period.

crop: An extension of the esophagus in a condor's throat in which food is held immediately after it is eaten.

DDE: Dichloro-diphenyl-ethylene, a toxic compound formed when DDT breaks down into its component parts.

DDT: Dichloro-diphenyl-trichloroethane, a chlorinated hydrocarbon compound used to kill insects; its use is illegal in the United States.

double-clutching: The laying of two sets of eggs in the same season; condors will produce a replacement egg if one is lost.

down: The soft feathers closest to a condor's body that keep it warm.

ecosystem: A unit of the environment, including both nonliving elements and the community of interrelated organisms within the area.

endangered species: An animal or plant that has been scientifically determined to be at risk of extinction in all or a significant part of its range within the foreseeable future.

Falconiformes: The order of birds made up of the daytime hunting raptors such as hawks, falcons, and eagles.

fledgling: A chick that has grown flight feathers and is able to fly.

forage: The act of looking for food.

Gymnogyps californianus: The scientific name for the California condor.

habitat: An area that provides the physical elements needed by a certain animal or plant species.

hierarchy: A social organization in which certain individuals are dominant over others.

imprinting: The process of a young bird forming its identity based on who cares for it in the nest.

inbreeding: The act of closely related individuals mating and producing offspring.

incubation: The process of keeping eggs at the proper state of warmth for embryos to develop and young to hatch.

juvenile: A condor under the age of six, having head and feathers colored differently from an adult.

mentor: A teacher or guide; young condors will rely on older birds to serve as mentors to teach them how to survive in the wild.

molt: The process of a condor losing its feathers and growing new ones; condors molt once every year.

pipping: The process of a chick breaking the shell of its egg and beginning to hatch.

Pleistocene: A period of geologic time that began 2 million years ago and ended 10,000 years ago.

population: The total number of individuals within a given area.

primaries: The outermost feathers on a condor's wings.

raptor: A bird, such as a hawk, falcon, or eagle, that kills prey with powerful feet and sharp talons.

roost: A tree or other place where condors rest, especially for the night or during harsh weather.

scavenger: An animal that looks for carrion to eat instead of hunting and killing prey.

species: A category of biological classification denoting a group of physically similar organisms that breed with each other.

tagging: Marking a condor with a plastic tag affixed to the wing in order to tell individuals apart.

teratorn: A prehistoric vulture that was the largest flying bird of all time.

thermal: A rising body of warm air.

threatened species: An animal or plant that has been scientifically determined to be likely to become endangered within the foreseeable future.

toxin: A chemical compound that can cause illness or death in a living organism.

urohydrosis: The act of a condor or other vulture depositing urine on its legs both to assist in evaporative cooling and to inhibit the growth of bacteria.

Vultur gryphus: The scientific name for the Andean condor.

Organizations to Contact

Center for the Reproduction of Endangered Species (CRES)
San Diego Wild Animal Park
Zoological Society of San Diego
PO Box 120551
San Diego, CA 92112-0551
Website: www.sandiegozoo.org/cres/condor.html

CRES is the research and conservation arm of the San Diego Zoo and San Diego Wild Animal Park. These facilities have been involved in condor conservation since the late 1970s, and today the Wild Animal Park plays a vital role in the California condor captive-breeding program. In 2000 the Wild Animal Park opened Condor Ridge, a two-acre exhibit featuring rare native animals such as condors, bighorn sheep, and black-footed ferrets.

Cleveland Metroparks Zoo
3900 Wildlife Wy.
Cleveland, OH 44109
Website: www.clemetzoo.com

The Cleveland Metroparks Zoo supports a program to reestablish the Andean condor in Venezuela. Visit its website to learn more about Andean condors and how researchers track them through the use of satellites.

Los Angeles Zoo
5333 Zoo Dr.
Los Angeles, CA 90027-1498
Website: www.lazoo.org/condorco.htm

Since 1982 the Los Angeles Zoo has been breeding condors for eventual release into the wild. Its website has up-to-the-minute statistics on wild and captive condor numbers, fact sheets, and a history of the condor recovery effort.

Peregrine Fund
566 West Flying Hawk Ln.
Boise, ID 83709
Website: www.peregrinefund.org

The Peregrine Fund is the most recent organization to begin breeding California condors; it manages the release site near the Grand Canyon in Arizona. Condors, along with a variety of raptor species, are on display to the public at the fund's facility, the World Center for Birds of Prey. Its website includes field notes and observations about condors in Arizona.

U.S. Fish and Wildlife Service
Ventura Fish and Wildlife Office
2493 Portola Rd., Suite B
Ventura, CA 93003
Website: www.fws.gov

The U.S. Fish and Wildlife Service manages the California condor recovery program and oversees all aspects of habitat protection, breeding, and releases.

Ventana Wilderness Society
PO Box 894
Carmel Valley, CA 93924-0894
www.ventanaws.org

The Ventana Wilderness Society is a private nonprofit organization that manages the release of condors in the Big Sur coastal area of California. Its website is updated monthly with field reports detailing the lives of these birds.

Suggestions for Further Reading

Books

Caroline Arnold, *On the Brink of Extinction: The California Condor*. San Diego: Harcourt Brace Jovanovich, 1993. Highlights the efforts to capture and breed the last remaining California condors.

Wayne Grady, *Vultures: Nature's Ghastly Gourmet*. Vancouver: Greystone Books, 1997. Provides information about the biology and behavior of New World and Old World vulture species, including both California and Andean condors.

Will Hobbs, *Maze*. New York: Morrow Jr. Books, 1998. A fictionalized account of a troubled teenager who meets a biologist working on a condor release project in Utah.

Ian McMillan, *Man and the California Condor: The Embattled History and Uncertain Future of North America's Largest Free-Living Bird*. New York: E. P. Dutton, 1968. Includes observations of the wild condor population remaining in the 1950s and 1960s and also recounts early conservation efforts in the Sespe Condor Sanctuary.

David Phillips and Hugh Nash, eds., *The Condor Question: Captive or Forever Free?* San Francisco: Friends of the Earth, 1981. Includes arguments opposing the capture of condors for captive breeding at a critical time in the history of the California condor recovery effort.

Alvin Silverstein, Virginia Silverstein, and Laura Silverstein Nunn, *The California Condor*. Brookfield, CT: Millbrook,

1998. Describes the decline in condor numbers and the efforts made to maintain condor populations.

Noel Snyder and Helen Snyder, *The California Condor: A Saga of Natural History and Conservation*. San Diego: Academic Press, 2000. A comprehensive account of condor conservation by biologists once involved in condor restoration efforts.

Periodicals

Bill Gilbert, "Why Don't We Pull the Plug on the Condor and Ferret?" *Discover*, July 1986. A thoughtful article debating the value of certain endangered species recovery programs.

Works Consulted

Books

Roger Caras, *Source of Thunder: The Biography of a California Condor*. Boston: Little, Brown, 1970. An account of the natural history of the condor as well as a fictionalized tale of the life of a condor.

Tim Clark, Richard Reading, and Alice Clarke, eds., *Endangered Species Recovery: Finding the Lessons, Improving the Process*. Washington, DC: Island, 1994. An explanation of the positive and negative aspects of recovery programs for various endangered species.

Carl Koford, *The California Condor*. New York: Dover Publications, 1952. The results of the first landmark comprehensive study of the condor's biology and behavior.

P. J. S. Olney, G. M. Mace and A. T. C. Feistner, eds., *Creative Conservation: Interactive Management of Wild and Captive Animals*. London: Chapman and Hall, 1994. Accounts of creative solutions to the management of endangered wildlife.

Dick Smith, *Condor Journal*. Santa Barbara, CA: Capra, 1978. Describes the author's many years of observing wild California condors.

Sanford Wilbur and Jerome Jackson, eds., *Vulture Biology and Management*. Berkeley and Los Angeles: University of California Press, 1983. A comprehensive volume covering the evolution, biology, and status of vultures worldwide.

Periodicals

Jeffrey P. Cohn, "Breeding Success." *Americas*, January/February 1990.

———, "The Flight of the California Condor: After More than a Decade of Captive Breeding, the Big Bird Is on a Trajectory Toward Recovery," *Bioscience*, April 1993.

———, "Saving the California Condor." *Bioscience*, November 1999.

Sally Ann Connell, "Condors Take a Shine to Mountain Hamlet." *Los Angeles Times*, September 16, 1999.

Kathi Diamant, "Condor Ridge: A Bird's-Eye Preview," *ZooNooz*, February 2000.

Jerry Ferrara, "Why Vultures Make Good Neighbors," *National Wildlife*, June/July 1987.

Chris Kahn, "Condors Getting Too Close to Folks," *Columbian*, July 23, 1999.

Tom Kenworthy, "Wary Arizonans Give California Condors a Chilly Reception," *Seattle Times*, August 18, 1996.

John Krist, "Lead Poisoning Threatens California Condor Comeback," *San Jose Mercury News*, August 16, 2000.

John Lang, "Caged: The Last Wild Condor." *U.S. News & World Report*, May 4, 1987.

Christopher Lewis, "Endangered and Embroiled: Controversy Continues to Beset Attempts to Save the Condor," *Sports Illustrated*, October 31, 1988.

Alan Lieberman, et al., "The First Experimental Reintroduction of Captive-Reared Andean Condors into Colombia, South America," *Proceedings*, 1991.

Vicky Meretsky et al., "Demography of the California Condor: Implications for Reestablishment," *Conservation Biology*, August 2000.

Joanna Miller, "Condor 'Preschool' Teaches Fear to Wildlife," *Los Angeles Times*, August 17, 1995.

Jamie Murphy, "Last Days of the Condor? North America's Biggest Land Bird in Trouble," *Time*, December 30, 1985.

Jerry Nachtigal, "Biologists' Efforts Are Flying High as the New Day of the Condor Dawns," *Los Angeles Times*, November 9, 1997.

Kim Peterson, "Wild Animal Park Gets Even Wilder," *San Diego Union-Tribune*, May 25, 2000.

Gary Polakovic, "After Bouncing Back from Near-Extinction, the Giant Carrion-Eaters May Be About to Reproduce in the Wild," *Los Angeles Times*, November 8, 1998.

Mary R. Pols, "Early Socializing by Released Condors Surprises Biologists," *Los Angeles Times*, April 16, 1996.

———, "Condor Conundrum: Plan to Reintroduce Endangered California Bird to Grand Canyon Area Angers Residents of Region, but a Compromise Is Reached," *Los Angeles Times*, April 28, 1996.

Cherri Senders, "El Condor Pasa," *Omni*, August 1987.

William Toone and Arthur Risser Jr., "Captive Management of the California Condor," *International Zoo Yearbook*, 1998.

U.S. Fish and Wildlife Service, *California Condor Recovery* (fact sheets), Hopper Mountain National Wildlife Refuge Complex, 2000.

———, *California Condor Recovery Plan* (pamphlet), 3rd rev., Portland, OR: 1996.

Michael Wallace, "Methods and Strategies for the Release of California Condors to the Wild," *Proceedings*, 1991.

Michael Wallace and Stanley Temple, "Releasing Captive-Reared Andean Condors to the Wild," *Journal of Wildlife Management*, July 1987.

Robert Weller, "Curious Condors Take Stroll into Visitors' Center," *Seattle Post-Intelligencer*, August 28, 1998.

Stanley Wiemeyer, et al., "Environmental Contaminants in California Condors," *Journal of Wildlife Management*, April 1988.

Todd Wilkinson, "Homecoming," *National Parks*, May/June 1996.

Michael Ybarra, "Is This Bird Worth $20 Million?" *Los Angeles Times*, Sept. 14, 1997.

Internet Sources

Peregrine Fund, "Notes from the Field," 2000. www.peregrinefund.org/notes_condor.html.

San Diego Zoo, Center for the Reproduction of Endangered Species, "Hatching" (fact sheet), 2000. www.sandiegozoo. org/cres/hatching.html.

Ventana Wilderness Society, "Notes from the Field," 1999. www.ventanaws.org/notes99.htm.

Index

Picture Credits

About the Author

Karen D. Povey received her bachelor's degree in zoology at the University of California, Davis, and is currently pursuing her master's degree in education at the University of Washington. She has spent her career as a conservation educator, working to instill in people of all ages an appreciation for wildlife. After many years of living in the San Francisco Bay Area, she has recently made her home in Washington, where she manages and presents live-animal education programs at Tacoma's Point Defiance Zoo and Aquarium. When not working with animals at the zoo, she enjoys sailing and traveling with her husband and spending time with their pet Clydesdales, Bernese mountain dogs, and cats.